A Humanist Science

A Humanist Science

Values and Ideals in Social Inquiry

Philip Selznick

With a Foreword by Martin Krygier

Stanford University Press

Stanford, California

Stanford University Press
Stanford, California

Printed in the United States of America on acid-free, archival-quality paper

Library of Congress Cataloging-in-Publication Data

Selznick, Philip, 1919-
 A humanist science : values and ideals in social inquiry / Philip Selznick ; with
a foreword by Martin Krygier.
     p. cm.
 Includes bibliographical references and index.
 ISBN 978-0-8047-5862-8
1. Social sciences--Philosophy. 2. Social sciences and ethics. 3. Humanism--
History. 4. Philosophy and social sciences. I. Title.
H61.15.S47 2008
300.1--dc22
                                    2008013390

Typeset by Bruce Lundquist in 11.5/14 Adobe Garamond

Contents

Foreword

PHILIP SELZNICK'S life's work is distinctive in character and distinguished in quality. That is equally true of this new book, *A Humanist Science*, both in its own right and for the underlying themes and implications of that larger body of work and thought, which it discloses, distills, and extends.

Selznick has been an eminent and influential thinker in a wide range of social scientific disciplines, among them organization theory, general sociology, sociology of law, and social philosophy. He has written on many subjects, and his ideas have undergone cumulative refinement and development. Nevertheless, his thought has a deep and sustained coherence. It is, however, a complex coherence, not that of someone with just one thing to say.

One aspect of this coherence lies in Selznick's evolving views of the proper character of social inquiry and of its proper focus. *A Humanist Science* is above all, and almost literally, a distillation of these views. The word "distillation" is important here. I doubt that many people reading his early work would have realized the extent to which many of the themes central to this one were already animating the particular discussions there. I'm not even sure that Selznick always knew it. Sometimes, however, reading a writer's works backward is revealing. Doing so today, one is struck by the remarkable extent to which Selznick's oeuvre continually plays on and develops a coherent range of deep themes.

The first stage of Selznick's intellectual development began shortly before the Second World War, with an intense period of political engagement in that improbably fertile womb of academic (and literary) productivity, the New York Trotskyist movement, its parties and party-lets, factions and fractions. From that engagement came several writings read by a small number of clever would-be, soon would-have-been, and then never-wanted-to-be revolutionaries. Out of it, too, came Selznick's lifelong concern with "the conditions and processes that frustrate ideals or, instead, give them life and hope."[1] Some of his erstwhile colleagues abandoned such concerns when they ceased to be Trotskyists. Selznick never did. In one way and another, they animated all his subsequent scholarly work, which began at the same time and, after the war, developed into classic contributions to the sociological theory of organizations and institutions (*TVA and the Grass Roots* [1947], *The Organizational Weapon* [1954], *Leadership in Administration* [1957]), and general sociology (*Sociology*, with Leonard Broom, seven editions).

In his second period, beginning in the mid-1950s, Selznick became a founding and prominent member of the law and society movement, and founder of the Law and Society Center (1961) and later the Jurisprudence and Social Policy (JSP) Program (1978) at the University of California at Berkeley. The JSP was the first Ph.D. program in an American law school and remains one of the very few. It was also distinctive among pioneering law and society endeavors in its determination systematically to marry philosophical and sociological insights with each other and apply them to matters of practical policy consequence. As Selznick put it at the time, its "stress on humanist scholarship distinguishes what we are about from recent precursors of JSP, including the law and society movement. . . . I believe we can and should have a larger aspiration—the clarification of fundamental values. For this, we must rely heavily on philosophical, cultural, and historical modes of inquiry."[2] In this period Selznick also published several important essays (particularly "Sociology and Natural Law" [1961]), and books (*Law, Society, and Industrial Justice* [1969] and *Law and Society in Transition: Towards Responsive Law* [1978, reprint 2001]), notable, among other things, for their explicit and pervasive interweaving of descriptive, analytic, normative, and policy-oriented concerns.

His third period, which includes the present volume, has been more reflective than investigative, and more wide-ranging in scale and scope than his earlier work. It began with his magisterial *The Moral Commonwealth* (1992), a work of social philosophy (or philosophical sociology) of extraordinary range, ambition, erudition, and richness, concerned to explore the sources of "moral competence" in persons, institutions, and communities. It is a remarkable feat of intellectual architecture, both in its internal combination of clarity and complexity, scholarship and originality, and as a kind of elaborate piece of intellectual bridge building, which spans and connects many topics and fields, in positive and normative sociology, political and moral philosophy, and much else.

Having finished that major work, Selznick felt there remained loose ends to be tied up: one more specific and substantive in concerns and the other more general and in part methodological, though method and substance are rarely far apart in his thinking. Some new substantive themes had begun to emerge during the writing of *The Moral Commonwealth* (though they were prefigured much earlier), having to do with the communitarian turn of his thought. He wanted to communicate these themes as much to a larger educated audience as to his peers. *The Communitarian Persuasion* (2002) was the result. And distinct from, though closely connected with, his views about the substance of social and political philosophy, Selznick also had long practiced and advocated an approach to thinking about social, political, legal, and moral matters that blended philosophy, particularly moral philosophy, and social thought in a way that came to form what he called "humanist science." The JSP was an example of this, but his canvas was always larger than law. The present work represents an attempt to distill the elements of that larger aspiration, exemplify it, sketch where it might lead, and recommend it. Again he has had in mind an audience of intelligent readers, going beyond academic specialists but including them as well.

AS ONE WOULD EXPECT from a sociologist of Selznick's eminence, all of his work is unmistakably sociological in provenance, perspective, and sensibility, but in all of it one sees signs—and over the last forty years those signs have become unambiguous and programmatic—that he has "an ecumenical view of that discipline,"[3] one that includes political, legal, and moral theory, with blurred boundaries not rigorously policed, which we are encouraged to cross.

In Selznick's hands, social theory is an integrative pursuit, committed to both the explanation and the evaluation of social phenomena. This inclusive aspiration is key, in opposition ("revolt" would be too harsh a word for Selznick's temperament but not too strong for his conviction) to the "academic myopia" that he attributes in large part to the "rampant multiculturalism in academic life."[4] Much as he admires academic disciplines, and clear though it is that he is by formation and intellectual character a sociologist, he laments that

the disciplines to which many of us have devoted our lives, into which we have socialized our students, have unfortunately become intellectual islands. These islands have their own jargon, their own culture, their own paradigms, their own ways of thinking. These self-reproducing disciplines have often stood in the way of serious engagement with major issues.

Of course, as Selznick is well aware, not everyone agrees. This is not news. When in 1969 he published *Law, Society, and Industrial Justice*, his first extended monograph on law, the legal sociologist Donald Black responded with an extended review, protesting that while this was splendid "sociological jurisprudence," "undoubtedly the most erudite and imaginative example of the natural-law approach to appear," it was not sociology of law, not science.[5] Selznick's response was one that the old common law might have called "confession and avoidance," and it is typical of his impatience with academic border patrols. Yes, he mixes sociology with jurisprudence, and with other normative disciplines as well, but why not? "It seems late in the day, after so much waywardness and so much sterility, to insist upon a full divorce of the theoretical and the practical. In social science, as elsewhere, we place our bets on the enterprise of self-correction, not on a claim to complete objectivity."[6] There is no evidence that his views on these matters have changed. Humanist science, and its offspring normative social theory, are not oxymorons but inescapable complements, often rejected, not much practiced, hard to do, but pregnant with possibility.

The key to "humanist science" is Selznick's long-adhered-to conviction that appreciation of the role and play of values and ideals in the world is central to social understanding: what they are, what they do, what threatens them, what protects and sustains them, what enables them to flourish. That means acknowledging them as proper objects of study, rather than mere epiphenomena of whatever is thought really to matter. It also requires identification of the values at stake in particular social processes, practices, and institutions; clarification of the nature of these values; understanding of what endangers them; and exploration of the conditions in which they might thrive.

Since concern with values is omnipresent in this conception of social science, a social scientist should be informed by traditions of philosophical thought less chary of dealing with values than is typical of some of the more positivistic conceptions of behavioral (and legal) sciences. On the other hand, since so much that is important about the play of values in the world is subject to variation and refracted through particular contexts, philosophical speculation needs to be anchored in an understanding of these matters of fact, contingency, and variety. And so social sciences.

And since Selznick's concern is not with values applied to just anything, but always ultimately as they affect human persons, the learning with which a social scientist needs to be familiar—in aid of "genuine understanding of human frailty, suffering, and potentiality"—will center upon those of the traditions of humanism, broadly conceived. The distinctive aim of humanist science, blending insights from these various sources so often separated, is "analytical and empirical study of ideals and virtues, understood as at once latent in and threatened by the vagaries of social life." It must be alive to "the wholeness and the complexity of human persons and the contributions that social inquiry can make to human well-being."

PART 1 of *A Humanist Science* fleshes out central elements of "the humanist imagination" and both characterizes and exemplifies what Selznick takes to be its preoccupations and spirit. Selznick draws attention to some classic contributions to the emergence and development of that imagination, to its complex character and multiple incarnations, and to distinctive concerns and insights to be found and generated there. At the same time that he reports some of the central themes and claims of humanist writings, he characterizes the "grain" of a style of thought, what those drawn to it are inclined to value and consider important to understand.

These broad-brush historical reflections draw with ease, eloquence, and confidence on a life of reading and thought. What is emphasized is not paraded for its own sake or just for the record but to illustrate the development and to exemplify the particular character of humanist concerns, viewpoints, and sensibilities that are also Selznick's own. They are called upon and fashioned to show how they have been and may be wedded to social investigation that is amply *scientific* without being reductively *scientistic*, and whose "chief concerns are (1) to identify distinctive or animating ideals and (2) to learn what conditions affect their realization."

In Part 2, "Realms of Value," this mode of investigation, "social science as moral inquiry," is then brought to bear on a range of "major topics in social science"—social order and moral order, humanist virtues, the morality of governance, rationality and responsibility, the quality of culture, law and justice—to show how these large topics might be illuminated by humanist science. More general implications for moral philosophy, social science, and public philosophy are explored in Part 3.

THIS IS AN IMPORTANT and intriguing work, from at least three points of view. The first is as evidence of a highly individual and uncommon mind and cast of mind at work, and reflecting on the product of a life of thought. The book not only commends but exhibits a distinctive intellectual and moral sensibility, as much as it develops arguments or garners evidence. That sensibility warrants attention, even apart from the observations and arguments it generates. At any time, Selznick's ways of thinking, refined and developed through a long life of sustained investigation, scholarship, erudition, and reflection, would be distinctive and of interest. They are all the more so today, since in many ways they run counter to the "spirit of the age." Selznick is no raging iconoclast, but *A Humanist Science* represents a style of enterprise that few modern thinkers would be able or willing to attempt. Implicit in Selznick's measured and ecumenical prose is a critique of much that is done by modern social scientists, on the one hand, and by philosophers, on the other. The work itself conforms to none of the hyper-specializations of late modernity, though it is not without respect for their achievements. With its roots in John Dewey's thought, and enriched by Selznick's own deep and long familiarity with an extremely rich range of thinkers from sociology, political science, psychology, philosophy, law, theology—the labels don't matter much to him—there are represented in these reflections a continuity and character of thought that have few parallels in the modern academy. Selznick is a thinker of significance, and such a distillation of some of his major commitments is to be welcomed, particularly since it is expressed with eloquence and grace.

A second virtue has to do with how we, not merely he, should go about thinking about the social, human world. For what Selznick represents is a point of view in modern social thought that deserves serious consideration in its own right. Many people admire the power of modern specializations, the skill involved, and the intellectual rewards to be gained. But, as some will acknowledge, all this cleverness comes at a price in terms of, among other things, intellectual and moral spaciousness, and largeness of concerns. I believe Selznick's book will remind most readers of some of the virtues of such spaciousness and reach, and also of what is lost when they are (as they often are) systematically, even proudly, reduced, and when methods replace problems as agenda-setters. Perhaps "remind" is too optimistic a word here. Social scientists under a certain age may well not have even encountered such virtues, let alone imagined that a card-carrying social scientist might hazard to exhibit them, and still less believe that they are central to his and their common vocation.

Selznick does believe this, and he argues for it, not as some plotless call for "interdisciplinarity" or "cross-disciplinarity" or even "transdisciplinarity" but rather as a demand that what we draw upon intellectually match the character and complexity of what we are trying to understand.

At a time when interdisciplinary research receives a good deal of lip service, and when there is danger (often realized) of sliding into undisciplined mush, Selznick's work is a reminder of what can be gained from such boundary-crossings and even blurrings, when they are sensitively and intelligently undertaken. This interdisciplinarity is partly just a necessary outgrowth of the largeness of Selznick's concerns, but it is also a product of considered reflection on what is necessary for us to understand and usefully affect complex social processes.

His determination to mix the concerns of social research and moral philosophy is rare among empirical social scientists, and the depth of his philosophical knowledge and insight is rarer still. It is not the way most social scientists have been trained, or think, today. Relatively few share his large view of the discipline or would know what to do with it. On the other hand, Selznick is a great sociologist and he is concerned with bringing to bear on normative, philosophical questions a close examination of social realities and a disciplined understanding of the way that complex and large social and political institutions work, and vary, in the world. Modern philosophers are commonly innocent of such matters.

Third, the book delineates for humanist science a subject with which we are all concerned but by which value-free social scientists are too often merely embarrassed. We are invited to treat as central the fate of values in the world and to learn to be alert—scientifically alert—to "recurrent sources of vitality and decay. This is an agenda for a humanist science of social life." The book is full of wise and thoughtful appraisals of what matters in social life, what leads to social flourishing, what sorts of conditions allow humans to thrive and what sorts diminish our chances. In all this, there is no shyness about exploring the *qualitative* differences among human experiences, differences that Selznick laments are of somewhat less concern in many of our ordinary social sciences than they are in most of our ordinary lives. Within a humanist science, this combination of facts and values, appraisals and recommendations, is in no way an embarrassment, as it is in so much behavioral science, where it commonly occurs anyway but coyly, *sotto voce*, even clandestinely. And there is a great deal here that would speak to an intelligent non-specialist more directly, insightfully, and helpfully than does standard-issue academic work.

Some readers will be impatient with this message, with this style of book, and indeed with the enterprise as a whole: not "cutting edge," not parading novelty, not advancing some revelatory new method or methodology, too vague, cloudy, hortatory, and so on. There is something in this sort of criticism, and perhaps it is why books of this sort are rarer than they once were. But it is not an accident that a great deal of modern social science deals with topics smaller in every sense than Selznick's, some so small as to be hardly visible. There is a great deal to be gained when a scholar of distinction chances his arm and extends his reach in the way that is done here. My own view is that any loss of "bite" or "rigor," in the modern behavioralist senses of these terms, is more than compensated for by the largeness, fineness, and richness of the enterprise.

As might be expected of someone who has been writing for well over sixty years, there is an autumnal tone to this book. It is not an attempt to plough new fields but rather to harvest what has been cultivated, and what might still and again bear fruit. It is not "original research" in the modern sense, nor indeed as most of Selznick's own earlier works were. This book is truly a distillation. But the particular distillation is new, clear, eloquent, fine—and frequently a delight to read. And, as always with Selznick, one senses that one is in the hands of a wise, humane, erudite, sane, and deeply reflective guide. His concerns may not always be our own, we needn't follow him everywhere, but it is hard not to learn from him. *A Humanist Science* is an elegant coda to a distinguished life of thought and a statement of an important intellectual position, today too rarely heard.

Martin Krygier

Preface

AT BOTTOM, this book argues for a closer connection between social science and the humanities, especially philosophy and history. My thesis is that social science is largely value-centered: economics, political science, social psychology, and sociology are preoccupied with ideals of rationality, legitimacy, self-government, personal development, and social cohesion. These disciplines call for close observation and dispassionate analysis of contexts and outcomes. Among the humanities, philosophy clarifies values and meanings while history identifies master trends, such as urbanization and industrialization, that affect values. Philosophy and history give direction to social science, but at the same time they are subject to criticism and revision in light of social science findings.

I have used these ideas regarding the play of values and ideals in social inquiry in several of my earlier works. In *TVA and the Grass Roots* I showed how an ideal of responsiveness was frustrated by local interests and ideologies. *Leadership in Administration* examined the value-centered work of institutional leaders in defining and protecting the character and direction of their organizations. In *Law, Society, and Industrial Justice* I studied how authority is limited by collective bargaining and workplace realities. *The Moral Commonwealth* sought to make clear the moral character of persons, institutions, and communities. In *The Communitarian Persuasion* I explored the meaning of community, with emphasis on diversity as well as cohesion.

This way of thinking owes much to my early study of pragmatist philosophy as presented in the writings of John Dewey. Dewey regarded the separation of fact and value as a "pernicious dualism." Values arise from factual conditions, he argued, and whether they are realized or not is also a factual matter. Dewey focused on consummations and frustrations, that is, on qualitative aspects of experience rather than content alone. The wants and needs of human beings cannot be attributed to a generic human nature; they are determined by specific settings. A link is thereby forged between the scientific demand for close observation and the values realized in social life.

I have called this book *A Humanist Science* in part to make clear the interdependence of fact and value. Facts are the conditions affecting human achievements; values are ideals realized or undermined by those conditions. A discipline that brings out this interdependence is a humanist science. My focus on the social sciences shows how ideals emerge from economic activity, the quest for justice, and the challenge of living a common life.

I begin in Part 1, "The Humanist Imagination," with a discussion of major strands of humanist thought, looking back to ancient Greece and the Renaissance. I note the centrality of ideals in nature and in human life. Part 2, "Realms of Value," argues that rationality, legitimacy, self-government, social cohesion, and authenticity are chief concerns of political science, economics, social psychology, sociology, and anthropology. Part 3, "Philosophy and Social Science," explores the bearing of the preceding discussion on naturalism in ethics and a pluralist vision of society. I conclude with some thoughts on social knowledge as the clarification and limits of ideals.

I WISH TO THANK MY WIFE, Doris R. Fine, for much emotional, practical, and intellectual support; also Martin Krygier, Michael J. Lacey, and Kenneth Winston for valuable comments and suggestions. I am also grateful for the able assistance of Ning Yu and Christie Lim.

P.S.

A Humanist Science

Part One   The Humanist Imagination

1

The Humanist Tradition

THE IDEA OF HUMANIST KNOWLEDGE goes back at least to the thought of Socrates, as presented in Plato's dialogues; it is prefigured in ancient religious ideas about human nature and the imperatives of a human life. The humanist *tradition* is or should be more definite than either of these; humanist *science* requires more direction and warrant. Like other moral and intellectual traditions, such as rationalism, romanticism, liberalism, and conservatism, humanism is a loosely woven fabric, composed of varied strands. As one or another strand predominates, a "new" humanism is proclaimed.

We need not be distracted by the many different voices that are prepared to say: "I too am a humanist." This claim has been made by Marxists, Catholics, and many students of "the humanities." Some historians have traced humanism to Renaissance thinkers, like Erasmus (1466–1536), who rekindled admiration for ancient Greece and Rome, brought to Europe a deep regard for learning, and used Latin to transcend national and linguistic boundaries. Today humanism is mainly associated with rejection of supernaturalism and with confidence in the human capacity to find moral truth without the aid of divine revelation.

There is substance in all these claims, but there is also a risk that humanism becomes so large a tent, so spacious an idea, as to lose all distinctiveness. Therefore we need to make plain the animating principles of the humanist vision. Here I emphasize the principles that lead to "humanist science." These have important connections to major themes in Western intellectual history: the ideas of Plato and Aristotle, Judeo-Christian beliefs, Renaissance art and learning, the Protestant Reformation, the Enlightenment project, nineteenth-century romanticism, historicism, and existentialism, twentieth-century thought, especially in cultural anthropology, and the humanist naturalism of American pragmatism. All have contributed to the humanist tradition; all have added genuine understanding of human frailty, suffering, and potentiality. Three main components of the humanist tradition are: (1) belief in and quest for objectively grounded moral truth about social and personal well-being, (2) liberation from ignorance, superstition, and uncritical acceptance of custom and authority, and (3) rejection of whatever threatens the wholeness and intrinsic worth of human persons.

The Examined Life

In Plato's *Apology* we learn of Socrates' thoughts after he was condemned to die for allegedly corrupting the youth of Athens. Invoking Apollo's creed,[1] Socrates says, "The unexamined life is not worth living."[2] The examined life is informed by our best efforts to know what virtue requires and what obstacles must be surmounted.

The Centrality of Ideals

In the Platonic vision, our lives should be governed by appropriate ideals or standards. We compare our choices, projects, and customs with the ideals to which they should aspire. For this we need sound knowledge of human virtues and the forms of life that lead to their realization or undoing. We must ask what is the distinctive excellence or virtue (*arete*) of a craft or institution, a son, father, mother, teacher, or ruler. The virtues are known by the ideals they foster and the excellences they demand. These are the criteria by which we judge what we do and how we think.

For Socrates, and more generally for Greek *paideia*, education is not an unreflective process of enculturation by which one generation exercises its power over a dependent and receptive successor. Rather, an ideal of critical inquiry prevails. We know it today as the ideal of liberal education.

Here we see, if only dimly, the chief feature of humanist science: analytical and empirical study of ideals, understood as at once latent in and threatened by the vagaries of social life. The ideals we should treasure are necessarily precarious, often frustrated or distorted by unwanted pressures and temptations. Yet they are also grounded in social experience—that is, in impulses, fears, hopes, and opportunities.

Ideals and Knowledge

The Greek preoccupation with ideals is accompanied by two doctrines that have long intrigued students of mind and nature. The first is Plato's strong contrast between a pristine, unchanging world of forms or ideas and a more clouded, elusive, less reliable world of perception and conduct that obscures the pristine realm. According to Plato, inconstancy is the hallmark of ordinary experience, whose underlying reality is veiled by uncertain images and filtered through the contingent circumstances of everyday life.[3] Since those experiences produce only appearances, they have dubious value as sources of knowledge. To achieve true knowledge, Plato tells us, we must leave the blinkered world of cave-dwellers and enjoy the sunlight of reason. Only pure intellect, undimmed by distorting senses, can reveal the *eidos*—the "form" or "idea"—that gives an object its special character. Truth is not fathered by our senses; instead, its parents are *reflection* and *analysis*, which must prevail. Everything worth knowing has an *eidos*, which, once discovered, permits us to clarify meanings and identify objects, for example as "portraits" or "landscapes." We thus discern the special qualities of justice, piety, love, or beauty. These "ideal types" are truer than perceptions of unanalyzed experience. In Platonic metaphysics there is no reality apart from the form that gives a phenomenon its name and nature.

A scientific or theoretical ideal loses its innocence and its moral neutrality when it becomes a basis for criticism and a guide to conduct.

Although in theory the Platonic doctrine speaks to all of nature, and the foundations of all knowledge, it comes into its own when human ideals and their vicissitudes are examined. The "ideas" of justice, piety, love, and beauty are normative as well as cognitive. The distinctive virtues of each are clarified, and standards leading to those virtues are fashioned. In effect, what was a device for advancing natural science becomes, for the moral philosopher, a vision of the good.

Greek Naturalism

Plato's great pupil, Aristotle, shared his master's view that moral ideals should be based on objective knowledge. However, he was more sensitive to and respectful of the texture, promise, and troubles of social life. For Aristotle, a central idea is *telos* or "end-state." The *telos* of a structure, process, or organism is an ideal condition that realizes special values and the capacity to survive and flourish. *Telos* is natural in that it draws on resources that the system itself produces. For Aristotle, as for Plato, an ideal is an animating principle, not a construct of the intellect; it is summoned and sustained, or threatened and impaired, by recognizably human desires and needs.

An example is physical and mental health, which necessarily includes standards of well-being. The *telos* of a person, a college, or a community is a state of well-being. The criterion of that state is some special competence, such as, for persons, emotional maturity; for schools, intellectual discipline; for families, care and commitment. To know a *telos* is to know the relevant ideals and the possible congenial or uncongenial conditions. This is where "nature" comes in.

For Aristotle, *eidos* and *telos* are related ideas. *Telos* without *eidos* is an incoherent notion because *telos* presumes or predicates *eidos*. An *eidos* cannot be realized or understood without knowing what human life makes possible and what it forecloses.

Seen in this light, "experience" is not flux and disorder. Instead, recurrent and orderly patterns are discovered. We can learn what ideals make sense in a given context, what disciplines they require, and what makes their realization possible, likely, or unlikely. In his *Politics*, Aristotle studied the variety of regimes and their significance for self-government and the abuse of power. This understanding of an empirical and grounded connection between ideals and realities is Aristotle's distinctive contribution to humanist thought.

Ideals and Self-Knowledge

When Socrates explored the nuances of virtue, he obeyed Apollo's dictum "Know thyself." At its core this doctrine is an ideal of humility. Visitors to Delphi were enjoined to remember that they were humans, not gods, and that they should not aspire beyond their limits. Only gods can do wonders; humans must learn the virtues of moderation, whether in drinking, fasting, or expressing emotions. Moderation was, however, a somewhat cramped understanding of what self-knowledge entails. A broader vision is found in the Greek commitment to self-awareness. "Know thyself" is more than a principle of restraint. It is a key to the human spirit. The virtues of humility and self-control may sometimes take quite primitive forms, such as unreflective subordination to rulers or priests. We should, instead, scrutinize the values that we cherish but only dimly understand and mindlessly defend. Socratic self-knowledge attends to nuance and irony, to meanings that reveal what ideals demand and what they cost.

Humanity Unchained

The Greek dedication to reflection and self-knowledge—especially in the legacies of Plato and Aristotle—gave great authority to philosophical learning and set standards for two millennia of humanist scholarship. The Greek texts honored rigorous thought about human nature, including its varieties and troubles.

This commitment to critical inquiry would, in time, weaken the authority of tradition. Although the main concern was human virtue, ideals of piety were also threatened. This was the charge against Socrates, a charge not without foundation. That reflection is dangerous and potentially subversive is a thought expressed, with characteristic eloquence, by Thomas Jefferson: "I have sworn upon the altar of God eternal hostility against every form of tyranny over the mind of man."[4] The chief source of this tyranny is the claim to a monopoly of truth and a right to suppress dissent.

Enlightenment Humanism

Eighteenth-century intellectuals in Europe and America, building on the earlier writings of Hobbes, Spinoza, Leibniz, Descartes, Luther, and Calvin, flocked to the banner of freedom. Liberties of conscience and expression were extolled: freedom is protected when people can think without constraint and speak without fear of political or clerical repression. "Man is born free," said Rousseau, "and he is everywhere in chains."[5] The most burdensome bonds are ignorance, superstition, and uncritical subordination. Enlightenment humanism sought to break these fetters and thereby reclaim an ennobling heritage. It expressed confidence in reason and regarded humans as rational beings, thus creating an icon of modernity. From now on, it was thought, the legitimacy of authority would depend on how well it was justified by the good sense of humankind. This outlook can be seen in the Protestant Reformation and its sectarian offshoots. Protestants of every stripe demanded freedom of conscience, belief, and worship. They argued that a public policy should respect the individual's quest for redemption. These claims led to a great flowering of theological discussion, which helped create a culture of disputation. People bowed to religious precepts and clerics; they welcomed enforcement of conventional morality. However, they also embraced the idea that religious identity is a *chosen* state of grace, a manifestation of the self-forming human spirit. At once critical and constructive, this doctrine became part of the humanist tradition. Renaissance humanists—Dante, Erasmus, Machiavelli, Spinoza—differed from earlier writers in thinking for themselves and seeking the support of an international community of independent scholars. They celebrated learning and unfettered thought, which required freedom from established authority. Although Enlightenment humanism[6] spoke loudly on behalf of the human spirit, its vision was dimmed by a fateful overreaching: rationality in human affairs was exaggerated, a defect that produced an intellectual upheaval in the nineteenth century as rationalism was offset by romantic and historical ideas.

The Menace of Abstraction

A basic failing of the Enlightenment project was its inability to grasp the concreteness and variety of human existence. The idea of humanity withers when a narrowed conception of reason becomes the chief virtue and main criterion of human achievement. Though an appeal to reason can be uplifting and ennobling, by itself it cannot do justice to the aspirations and sufferings of humanity, and especially the human need for attachment and identity. As the humanist tradition developed, it came to embrace some of the Enlightenment perspectives. *Sapere aude*— "dare to know"—was a motto of Immanuel Kant. Yet humanism had to distance itself from ideas that derogated tradition, passion, and sentiment and that celebrated only rational choice and logical argument. For some humanists, Enlightenment philosophy was more menacing than attractive. The abstractions of the Enlightenment could not see the value of diversity or appreciate the knotty texture of the social fabric.

"Glory be to God for dappled things."[7] This pious verse gave thanks for "pied beauty"—that is, for a mixed and multifarious natural world. Gerard Manley Hopkins saw beauty in open fields and the flourishing abundance of species and habitats. He saw divinity vividly displayed in brambled hillsides, self-renewing pastures, and virgin woodlands, not in unvarying stands of wheat or other single-species crops. In a theological idiom, God's plenitude is a humans-friendly world, where people can feel at home and live in full awareness of diversity in unity. A yearning for concreteness and the diversity it brings is at the core of the humanist tradition.

Organic Unity

Some humanist writers have relied on the concept of organic unity to explain what they have in mind. This idiom is sometimes explicit, as in the writings of Samuel Taylor Coleridge,[8] but more often "organic unity" is an implicit idea, not very clear or well understood. It is, however, a key to the humanist ethos.

Organic unity is readily apparent in biological systems that experience growth, adaptation, and close integration of structures and functions. The parts are connected to each other and help sustain a living whole. Applied to social life, the idea of organic unity points to vital structures and processes such as the creation of persons, beliefs, communities, and cultures. All are mainly products of adaptation and self-renewal; they are not necessarily *designed* or purpose-driven. Human persons, for example, are formed by unchosen relationships and unplanned interactions. Habits, attitudes, and self-conceptions are formed, which in time distinguish individual beings. Yet selves and identities are only more or less well integrated; they are sometimes riven by enduring conflicts. Human personalities are not assembled mechanically like clocks or computers. Rather, they are formed by unique histories of attachment or trauma.

We should distinguish *organic* unities from other unities, such as rationally designed systems of coordination and cooperation. The latter may be held together by specific benefits or by coercion and command. These are indeed kinds of unity, but they are not *organic* unities. The latter draw on quite different sources of stability and cohesion, including shared beliefs and practices. The prize sought is more than bare survival or minimal levels of incentive and morale. Organic unities often supplement more artificial or mechanical forms of integration. Both kinds of unity abound, and both are needed. A major challenge for science and policy is to learn how mechanical and organic unities interact and support one another.

Although the term "organic unity" has a positive connotation, negative examples may be found in the form of "organizational cultures" that produce tunnel vision, turf battles, and other forms of disarray. For example, an intelligence agency may be guided by beliefs that hinder analysis or frustrate the sharing of vital information. Another example is the search for coherence in a constitution or a complex statute. Some such documents do not contain explicit principles; in fact, they may be little more than lists of particular powers or procedures, and thus they may offer inadequate guidance for interpretation and enforcement. Organic unities are fostered by explicit statements of purpose and principle, often in an introduction or preamble. In American constitutional history, the Declaration of Independence has sometimes served as an authoritative guide to interpreting the Constitution (drafted eleven years later), thus lending the Constitution greater moral and political coherence.

Insofar as there is organic unity—in a particular person, family, community, or work of art—it is not a mere means to particular ends. Rather, organic unities have "intrinsic" worth. They are valued for the direct satisfactions they bring or for other benefits they provide, such as "the rule of law" and "federalism." In organic unities, "purpose" yields to "function" and "system." This transition does not derogate ideals. On the contrary, people who participate in organic unities or study their troubles or try to control them pay close attention to the state of the system, especially its ability to care about the *quality* of a marriage, family, friendship, or community. The ideal is an ensemble of virtues that affect the ability of the system to take advantage of opportunities and devise strategies for self-improvement and repair.

Resistance to Abstraction

A leitmotif of the humanist tradition is concern for the integrity of organic unities as embodied in distinctive histories. Organic unities are compromised or destroyed when they are treated as instances of abstract categories or as tools for the advancement of larger objectives. In his theory of morality, Kant argues that human beings should always be treated as ends in themselves and not as "means only."[9] Kant did not say that a person's work or thoughts should never be means to other ends. Rather, people should never be treated as means *only*. We adhere to this principle when we insist that mechanical or rational systems should respect the just claims of persons and other organic unities. This ideal is prominent in the history of humanist thought. In his early so-called humanist writings, Karl Marx treated "alienation" as a human cost of factory work.[10]

His theory of self-estrangement was part of a broader intellectual current, which rejected the rationalist and atomistic doctrines of the seventeenth and eighteenth centuries. Instead, nineteenth-century thinkers like Marx regarded rationalism as a destructive virus composed of pernicious abstractions. In this view, rationalism sunders the unities that sustain cultures and removes meaning from life. Deprived of anchors and cut loose from moorings, people lose their humanity. The integrity of persons (and their organic unities) is threatened when organic unities are weakened by self-annihilating abstraction—that is, when persons, groups, institutions, and communities are detached from settings that give them distinctive qualities as well as support. Nineteenth-century philosophers and historians called for a "return to the concrete." This became a notable theme in European phenomenology and existentialism, as well as in American pragmatism. Resistance to abstraction has been a basic teaching of the humanities, especially history, literature, and the arts. General insights derive from the explanation of uniqueness. The German historian Leopold von Ranke said history should describe "*wie es eigentlich gewesen war*" ("the way things actually were").[11] The humanities convey general truths about the experience of being human, but these insights are grounded in the concreteness of poetry, sculpture, beliefs, and architecture. It is a staple of criticism in the arts to ask, Does the artist bring out the uniqueness and complexity of the object? This is an appeal to latent abstractions, that is, to the message contained in a work of art. There can be no message without abstraction; yet the quest for principles that give coherence to organic virtues is unending.

The chief drawback of abstraction is that it limits perception of individuality and intrinsic worth. Humanists recoil from the "abstract individual" and resist classifying people as consumers, employees, citizens, or welfare recipients. Instead, they prize an exuberant plurality, welcoming many different ways of being human and forming beliefs and identities. This attraction to diversity stems from a belief that rootedness is a foundation of human well-being; that a good life depends on strong attachments to kin, place, and occupation. These attachments create the diversity that we acknowledge and respect.

Humanist Naturalism

In twentieth-century philosophy a humanist perspective is well expressed in the writings of John Dewey (1859–1952). Dewey's philosophy is wholly naturalist in spirit and substance, yet it is well within the humanist tradition. At bottom is Dewey's conception of "nature." Although fully committed to the ideals and logic of science, Dewey rejected a view of nature as mainly manifest in abstract laws or principles. He argued for a "natural history," which perceives nature in the profusion of mountains, rivers, forests, and species. For Dewey, nature is a realm of events, individualities, latencies, and fulfillments. These he called "generic" features of the natural world—a world experienced by humans and informed by their sensibilities, needs, and hopes. Nature is never fully described or explained by the laws and principles of biology, chemistry, and physics. Rightly understood, nature is concrete, not abstract—a concreteness that summons awe, humility, fear, and love. According to Dewey, nature is "pregnant with connections" among realities and potentialities, species and environments, kin and colleagues. These connections create worlds of cooperation, competition, and interdependence—all supported by feelings of belonging and of rivalry. Dewey thought we should understand nature as it impinges on human life, and this theme gives his naturalism a distinctively humanist character. This becomes more pronounced in his treatment of such topics as growth, adaptation, and intelligence—all part of the effort to deal with "problems of life."

Humanist naturalism is surely "anthropocentric," but it makes no claim to human self-sufficiency. Rather, it places man *in* nature, not above nature or in opposition to nature. There is no question of "conquering" nature or failing to recognize human dependency or shortsightedness. Another aspect of humanist naturalism is that it encourages an ecological imagination. In contemporary ecology, "nature" is understood as "natural history." It is experienced concretely and appreciated for its diversity, interdependence, and self-renewal. This viewpoint runs counter to Enlightenment science, which is largely indifferent to environmental protection and the fate of nonhuman species. Ecologists care about the organic unities we call "ecosystems." The principles of heredity and competition may be abstractly formulated, but it is not forgotten that each ecosystem has its own worth as a habitat and its own imperatives of climate, soil, and space. Ecological sensibility is a contemporary manifestation of humanist naturalism.

The Paradox of Humanism

Humanists embrace particularity and value diversity. However, they do so in the name of more comprehensive ideals. A universalist impulse is combined with a perceived primacy of particular forms of life. Humans and other animals are valued for themselves; each has intrinsic worth and therefore cannot be a mere means to other ends. This premise rests on an even more fundamental ideal: that human experience, in its particularity, is a mainstay of well-being and a vital expression of the human condition. The primacy of the particular is neither self-evident nor self-justifying; it does not trump every other value. In fact, it may be compatible with subordination or self-sacrifice. Families and friendships have intrinsic worth insofar as they contribute to the quality of life.

To make this case we have to deploy fairly abstract ideas, e.g., that a person's "humanity" is expressed by ideals of caring and responsibility. An understanding of what "humanity" means is presumed, including potentialities and ideals, together with sobering truths about frailty, corruption, and propensities for destruction and self-destruction. According to this theory, human potentials and troubles are spurs to self-scrutiny and self-improvement. Although humanists have mostly had an affirmative view of human nature, they have also been aware of a darker side, which supports theological conceptions of finitude, sin, and the need for redemption. Ideas about the ways by which people and institutions go wrong are not difficult to find, as in theories of the abuse of power and corruption of the rule of law. Although judges and other officials accept an ethic of evenhandedness, justice is only partially blind to circumstances, such as the wealth or power of a litigant or defendant. The facts of a particular case are relevant, and rules are invoked to justify or excuse unlawful conduct. Such complexity makes a system of rules less rigid and more humane.

A similar paradox is found in the arts. The best literature, painting, or music conveys a general idea—a vivid expression of love, despair, or hope. The ideal product, however, is manifested in a particular work of poetry, narrative, drama, music, or sculpture. George Orwell's *1984* is memorable because the novel says something general about politics and propaganda but does so in and through descriptions of concrete events and attitudes. History is most compelling when it reaches beyond narrative to reveal master trends or principles. A creative union of the abstract and the concrete is the distinctive achievement and special pride of "high art." The promise of humanism is redeemed, not in particularity alone but in the concrete representation of general truths.

2

The Postulate of Humanity

THERE HAS LONG BEEN EVIDENCE of a "humanist underground"[1] in contemporary social science—an undercurrent of resistance to theories and methods that fail to grasp or stubbornly ignore both the wholeness and the complexity of human persons and the contributions that social inquiry can make to human well-being. The remedy for this resistance is a postulate of humanity, which in modern sociology is most apparent in studies of delinquency and other forms of "deviance." The message is that a nonconforming individual is "one of us," a person whose motive is understood and who deserves our respect. Most deviants are, in most ways, like everyone else. Although they experience different pressures, have different constraints and opportunities, and may live in distinctly different social worlds, their responses do make sense, not only to them but to the rest of us as well. The postulate of humanity makes for richer and more accurate descriptions, better explanations, and better policies.

The postulate reaches well beyond the study of deviance. It has been a major theme in the history of the social sciences and shows how those disciplines connect to the humanities. In the twentieth century that humanist voice was stilled by a dominant "scientism." Nevertheless, a humanist impulse remained, affirming the view that social science should do full justice to the subjectivity, particularity, plurality, and historicity of human existence. The postulate also shows how differences are transcended and how ideals arise from recurrent needs and strivings.

Taking ideals seriously requires unflinching realism; it is not an invitation to utopian fantasy. Ideals are subject to distortion and corruption, and they have strengths and weaknesses, which can be known only by objective and empirical inquiry.

A Great Divide

Early modern history combined love of learning with exuberant creativity in scholarship and the arts. Widespread knowledge of Latin helped to produce an international community of educated men, whose thoughts and writings rekindled interest in the philosophy and culture of the ancient world. Early modern humanists took for granted the centrality of man within a world not of his making. By the seventeenth century, however, notably in the writings of Benedict Spinoza, a personal and all-powerful God was displaced by more abstract conceptions of divinity, nature, and humanity. The pursuit of learning led to new expressions of pride and self-confidence. By Isaac Newton's time, "natural philosophy" came into its own, and brought new luster to mathematics, physics, and astronomy. There was reason to hope that one day quite soon the cosmos would be fully comprehended.

Yet there was a sobering downside: a knowable firmament, beyond human horizons, cast doubt on the centrality of *Homo sapiens*. The species could not remain "lord of creation." But glory could be found in scientific exploration. The new learning brought in its train a wealth of inventions and discoveries. This encouraged eighteenth- and nineteenth-century thinkers to envision a new science of mankind, one that would emulate natural philosophy by discovering the laws that govern man and society. Philosophers would dare to learn what "nature" allows and what it compels.

God was not forgotten, but His will, it was thought, was not arbitrary or inscrutable. Divinity was found in an orderly nature; and humans were ennobled by uncovering the secrets of the cosmos.

Kant's Road Map

In the late eighteenth century everything was made plain—or so it seemed for a time—by the philosophy of Immanuel Kant (1724–1804). Kant's ideas greatly influenced nineteenth-century thinking about ethics and science, especially in establishing a great divide between the sciences of physics, astronomy, and mathematics and the "human" or "moral" sciences of history, politics, and economics.

Kant upheld Newtonian science but left room for an intellectually respectable realm of faith, selfhood, and morality. He made a fundamental distinction between a world of "appearances" and a different ("noumenal") world of true reality. Appearances are not necessarily ephemeral or lawless. They can be systematically noted and carefully analyzed, and they can tell us a great deal about fields like biology, mechanics, and astronomy. However, such inquiries cannot reveal "things in themselves"—the reality behind appearances. This limitation does not affect the validity of Newtonian science because appearances are objective indications of an underlying reality. Kant's conception of a "noumenal" world, beyond appearances, ensures the objectivity and the truth-value of natural science. The world of appearances is necessarily "constructed" by the a priori concepts and categories of our minds. Without these presuppositions, we could not apprehend objects, sequences, or causes; we could not perceive extension or temporality. The phenomenal world studied by natural science rests on the powers and limits of the human mind. Nevertheless, the noumenal world of true reality, though inaccessible to science, can be reached by a different kind of inquiry, which brings faith and freedom into play and which is value-centered and spiritually informed. In this noumenal realm we go beyond "understanding" (*Verstand*) to "reason" (*Vernunft*). Kant made room for faith and for another kind of knowledge, different from natural science, which would discern the truths of that other realm, which was based on reason and fortified by faith. This perspective opened new vistas for imagination, insight, and self-understanding.

Kant could not anticipate, still less control, the responses of his own and succeeding generations of European intellectuals. In the years following his death in 1804, Enlightenment rationalism lost much of its hold on a still-forming modern mind. A "counter-Enlightenment" gave prominence to very different ideas. Johann Gottfried Herder and Georg Wilhelm Friedrich Hegel found moral worth and historical significance in the shared consciousness created by custom and history, thus adopting more organic and holistic ways of thinking. Resisting atomistic conceptions of man and society, they objected to the idea that individual choice is the key to social arrangements for the pursuit of individual self-interest. Instead, they were drawn to self-determination and self-realization. Moving beyond the virtues of rationality—which they refused to identify with "reason"—they looked to the historical and emotional attachments that supplemented, modified, and sometimes reinforced the pursuit of collective self-interest.

Thus individualism was disparaged in favor of interdependence, co-operation, and good order. The "counter-Enlightenment" thinkers found much refreshment in Kant's idea of a "noumenal" or "true" reality, unknowable to physical science but graspable by a more searching and subjective inquiry. This was an inviting prospect for *neo*-Kantians, who gave Kant's doctrines their own spin and drew their own conclusions. Most important was their vision of *Geisteswissenschaften* or "sciences of spirit." Strong voices in historical study (such as Wilhelm Dilthey, Max Weber, and Georg Simmel) entered the conversation, arguing that the human sciences—history, political science, sociology, psychology, economics, jurisprudence, and anthropology—differ in fundamental ways from the physical sciences. The human sciences can and do provide knowledge of human nature and social life, but this must include the worth and limits of freedom, rationality, and self-transcendence.

Inwardness

According to the post-Kantian thinkers, the human sciences take seriously the subjectivity and historicity of experience. This inward turn meant that the human sciences necessarily study how people feel, perceive, evaluate, and interpret; how selves are formed and refashioned; how people experience authority and cooperation—in short, how they govern lives lived in association with others. Once the genie of conscious-ness was out of the bottle, the *history* of consciousness became a leading topic, which could only gladden the hearts of thinkers who readily associ-ated consciousness with ideas, and therefore with what they most loved and best understood.

As this development shows, and as many scholars have observed, Kant must be seen as a transitional figure. He was, to be sure, a vigorous proponent of Enlightenment ideas. Embracing the motto *sapere aude* ("dare to know"), he prized moral autonomy and rejected unreflective obedience to a received or imposed morality. Kant's contribution to European thought, as it developed in the nineteenth century, included his proposal that the study of subjectivity include *ideals* as well as *ideas*. Subjectivity was no stranger to the Kantian system. It was, indeed, a foundation of his epistemology, whose central teaching is the creative, object-forming work of the human mind. In Kant's ethics, moreover, a subjective condition—goodwill—is the supreme virtue of man and the best guarantor of right conduct.

A turn toward inwardness is easy to find in the writings of He-gel, Marx, Dilthey, Weber, Dewey, and James. In Hegel's *Phenomenology of Spirit* transformations of consciousness are chief themes. Karl Marx took a similar path in his preoccupation with class-consciousness and in his writings on alienation. Dilthey explicitly associated the human sciences with *Verstehen* or intersubjective meanings. Weber also advo-cated a *verstehende Soziologie* and applied that doctrine in his study of the capitalist "spirit" as it emerged from the theological doctrines of Calvin and Luther. William James saw subjectivity as the key to understanding how people create and encounter their social worlds. These perspectives echo and amplify Kant's cognitive subjectivism, which became, in other hands, a more robust and comprehensive postulate of humanity.

The Human Good

Kant's idea of a "noumenal" realm, "intelligible" to reason but inac-cessible to science, spurred an even more radical subjectivism. If reason apprehends moral, aesthetic, and religious truth, a new light shines in the noumenal darkness. The human mind becomes something more than a filter and source of order in the "phenomenal" world of "appearances." The noumenal realm is opened up, if not to physical science then to a different way of arriving at spiritual truth. This project requires analysis of subjective experience, including the "goodwill" that one brings to issues of duty and obligation. As a result, new ways of thinking and feeling are legitimated. The postulate of humanity becomes an opening to the heart.

The inward turn is by no means morally neutral. It leads, on the contrary, to more searching and sensitive judgments. Spiritual well-being becomes the main criterion of health and goodness.[2] To look closely at "lived experience" (*Erlebnis*) is to scrutinize and assess states of mind and spirit: anxiety, autonomy and self-realization, the varieties of self-interest, the obligations of belonging—in short, what it means to live a fully human life.

"Spirit" has positive connotations of reflection and transcendence, of moral, aesthetic, and intellectual creativity. This affirmative view of human consciousness was taken for granted by those who explored the vicissitudes of *Geist* in society and history. They looked to human aspirations and achievements rather than to frailties or demonic impulses.

Some of the post-Kantian writers brought to the study of consciousness a fresh emphasis on contingency, variation, and development. They saw forms of consciousness as products of history, some more wholesome and empowering than others, some self-limiting or destructive.

This concern for the variability and quality of consciousness signaled a transition from *mind* to *self*. Whereas Kant stressed the structured perceptions of human minds, later writers adopted a vocabulary of selfhood and meaning. Such terms as "alienation," "self-determination," "authenticity," and "self-realization" added new dimensions of moral awareness to theories of consciousness.

Dilthey's Postulate of Humanity

A preeminent philosopher of the human sciences in the nineteenth century was Wilhelm Dilthey (1833–1911). Much preoccupied with foundational issues of subjectivity and historicity, Dilthey was sensitive to the values at stake in social life. The human sciences, he said, must study meanings and motives, and use interpretive methods. Otherwise, no description can be accurate or complete, no explanation can be valid, and no claim to empiricism can be justified. A human science true to itself will explore the ideals, strivings, failures, and fulfillments of everyday life.

"Life," or "lived experience," was thought to be the chief and proper subject of the human sciences. Moreover, human experience is active, need-reducing, and problem-solving. The goodness and quality of life cannot be ignored. In this respect, Dilthey was a significant precursor of American pragmatism.

The stress on subjectivity could license a view of human history as wholly determined by will and perception. But neither Dilthey nor Weber went down that road. For Dilthey, the social world enters into and is in part created by arrangements that limit what we can know and do. Dilthey favored a union of idealism and realism, and Weber's interest in subjective states did not interfere with realistic appraisals of power, status, interest, and domination. Different understandings of rationality, legitimacy, or religious doctrine led to different conceptions of authority and divinity.

Taking humans seriously and realistically respects their individuality and dignity and takes into account their varying needs, preferences, hopes, and fears. The injunction "take the point of view of the actor" is in part a moral message: remember the humanity of all persons, the despised as well as the honored; explore the conditions that help them resist degradation and oppression. A postulate of humanity directs inquiry to the moral promise of human life, including latent ideals of responsibility and cooperation. The betrayal or debasement of those ideals weakens solidarity and leads to disarray.

Spiritual Well-Being

In the Buddhist tradition a quest for "enlightenment" is the core of religious experience. Religion is about selfhood, not God; salvation is won by a regimen of self-discovery, not by worship of supernatural beings. This perspective is not very different from that implicit in other religions, which demand self-discipline and the construction of a self that is perceived as "holy," dedicated to ideals of sacrifice and obedience. The goal is spiritual well-being, which is more a psychic state than a particular set of beliefs and rituals. Religion heightened by personal dedication is rooted in conceptions of what humans can do, if they work at it, to reach a certain kind or level of consciousness. In this process, an ideal self judges a contingent or phenomenal self, which is subordinated to a controlled self and requires sustained self-scrutiny and dedicated instruction.

In Buddhism, spiritual well-being has clear moral dimensions: compassion for others and reverence for life. This is reflected in the Christian ideal of the "law of love." However, spiritual well-being may have demonic aspects, such as hatred of apostates or an inclination to wage holy wars. These darker passions distort, but do not change, the experience of spiritual well-being.

Spiritual well-being is a psychic state and involves a struggle to overcome distractions of desire and egotism, which are cognitive as well as moral. It helps overcome temptations of lust and self-dealing; it is suggested by feelings of compassion and sympathy. The mythic elements of religion are less important than practices that enlarge the communicant's ability to combine attachment with objectivity, sympathy, and judgment. These capacities are spiritual in that they center on feelings and dispositions. In this view, religion is about selfhood, not God.

History and Destiny

For the human sciences, as envisioned by Dilthey and other nineteenth-century thinkers, history has "meaning." Past events and trends are not indifferent to human needs and purposes. They contain intimations of fate and clues to destiny. Creation myths, for example, project a view of God as attentive to humanity. Such ideas endow a brutish, short-lived animal species with ancestral continuity and moral vision. The destiny of humankind becomes a chief anxiety, subject to earnest inquiry into the human condition. The stargazers ask: Why are we here? What is in store for us? What is our destiny?

Until modern times, the centrality of humankind could be taken for granted, but that attitude became untenable as science advanced. How could the accidental inhabitants of a small planet orbiting an unremarkable star think they were unique beneficiaries of divine creation? They could not see themselves as lead actors in a God-centered drama of sin, grace, judgment, and redemption.

These were daunting issues, but good news was waiting in the wings. The course of history might make sense after all; human pride could be salvaged. The seventeenth and eighteenth centuries promised rich compensation for the loss of cosmic centrality: confidence in reason—that is, in *human* reason. Properly educated and released from superstition, people can and will shape their own destiny. The name of that destiny is *progress*.

A few indulged in speculative excess and intellectual overreaching. Hegel saw progress in transformations of consciousness—a dream of reason in social life. Auguste Comte had his own vision of the history of consciousness: a progressive movement from theological and metaphysical thought to scientific ideas and attitudes. Herbert Spencer found progressive social evolution in the increasing complexity, differentiation, and reintegration of society. For Karl Marx social progress was rooted in economic circumstances, especially in the means of production. An increasing concentration of capital, together with advances in technology and organization, would create social conditions favoring class struggle and a socialist outcome. Nineteenth-century anthropologists found evolutionary patterns in facts detached from their contexts and arranged according to preconceived stages of development. Such claims tarnished the idea of social evolution, and generations of students have been taught to scorn these ideas as naive and wrong.

The critique of social evolution has not ended the search for master trends, nor has it relegated all nineteenth-century theories to the dustbin of historical scholarship. For example, Sir Henry Maine's argument, in *Ancient Law*, that "the movement of the progressive societies has hitherto been a movement *from Status to Contract*,"[3] is still an instructive theory, even though it must be qualified to take account of more recent trends.

Much the same may be said of master trends, such as Durkheim's idea that "organic" solidarity replaces "mechanical" solidarity; the transition from *Gemeinschaft* to *Gesellschaft*; Daniel Bell's theory of "post-industrial" society; and the trends that we call urbanization and secularization. These theories are subject to criticism and amendment, taking into account limiting contexts and countervailing trends. They are not expressions of revealed truth, nor do they claim the cachet of a philosophy of history. They are best understood as describing the contexts that govern many institutions and practices.

Nor do master trend theories derogate or ignore the choices people make. As Marx and Engels put it, "Men make their own history, but they do so within the conditions they encounter." Master trends limit choice, but no outcome is inexorable. They tell us what will happen if history is allowed to follow a line of least resistance.

The most important master trends are those that affect the high states or excellences of human life: success or failure in child rearing, the arts, education, or government. The values that inform these activities are precarious, subject to attenuation or distortion by ambient temptations. Precarious values need sustained nurture and special support. At stake are ideals of autonomy, self-mastery, caring, commitment, compassion, creativity, and authenticity. The preoccupations are plainly humanist: how people grow, mature, and flourish; how they create and sustain life-affirming institutions and life-enhancing relationships.

The phrase "master trend" is more neutral than "progress," less freighted with prejudgments. Yet a preoccupation with direction remains, especially the effects on human needs and satisfactions. *History* becomes *destiny* as the postulate of humanity guides questions put and answers received.

In a meditative conclusion to the second volume of *Democracy in America*, Alexis de Tocqueville portrayed a world transformed by insistent demands for equality—that is, for the elimination of inherited privilege and property. He saw the drive for equality as a problematic master trend, at once full of promise and fraught with peril. This attention to peril as well as promise distinguishes Tocqueville from theorists of progress, but not from prophetic ideas of destiny. History or destiny sets problems, offers opportunities, and expects judgment. The past is prologue in a drama as yet unfinished and unstaged. In this view, history reaches beyond study of the past to include what is significant for the future of human life.

A contemporary example is the sense we make of national sovereignty within a world made small by speedy communication and travel, and where human rights and rule-of-law ideals have urgent relevance. These conditions result in a waning of sovereignty. If rulers abuse their power in egregious ways, against their own people or others, it is increasingly likely that more universal norms will override traditional concepts of sovereignty and self-determination. Self-determination speaks more clearly to the rights and claims of groups, individuals, and families than to those of national governments. An international community makes itself felt by articulating and enforcing principles of just governance and better ways of resolving conflicts.

If the idea of sovereignty is losing its hold on the moral imagination, something important is said about the destiny of nations, even where local autonomy is privileged as the best way to correct the mistakes and follies of political leaders, or where ungoverned populism and manipulated opinion prevail. Destiny is manifest in inescapable troubles and limited options.

A Spacious Naturalism

The postulate of humanity points to a fundamental difference between humanist social sciences and physical or biological sciences. But we should ask what these social sciences have in common. What presuppositions do they share? Of course all are scholarly; all are committed to dispassionate study; all are supposed to eschew wishful thinking, intellectual arrogance, bad logic, and sloppy research. Is there anything special about a humanist *science*? Can we recognize the unity of all inquiry while blurring the line between science and philosophy, history, or literature? All of these disciplines may manifest a scientific *spirit*, committed to seeking objective knowledge, of, say, poetry, or history.

These reflections do not reject a scientific ethos, founded in clear public standards and theoretically grounded explanations of recurrent observations. On the contrary, they encourage it. A theory-centered ethos spurs the search for elementary components and fundamental principles. It has been said, with much justification, that a hallmark of the scientific ethos is "reducing the degree of empiricism."[4] The subject of inquiry, whatever it may be, has a "nature" revealed by distinctive "laws" or "principles." A scientific ethos, empirical as well as theoretical, is wholly committed to testing hypotheses and revising theories. Scientific assertions are warranted, not by logical exercises alone but also by repeated and repeatable observations.

Empiricism is nurtured by a naturalist philosophy—that is, by assumptions about what Dewey called the "generic" features of natural phenomena.[5] These include plural and contingent kinds, including rudimentary and developed forms. Hence *variation* and *contingency* are expected aspects of scientific inquiry.

In what used to be called the "moral sciences"—social science informed by moral philosophy—we recognize kinds of self-interest, love, consent, and choice, along with different kinds of authority or punishment. The differences are revealed by factual inquiry, not by the reflections of closet scholars, however insightful or astute they may be. Empiricism conveys the salutary message that analytical distinctions do not preclude empirical and contingent connections.

The meaning of empiricism is broadened, and its mandate is enlarged, by a spacious naturalism. In this view, no part of nature is inaccessible to knowledge. Human strivings and sufferings are part of nature, as are their vulnerabilities and strengths, successes and failures, fulfillments and frustrations. All are knowable, as are their conditions and contexts; all are sustained or undone by congenial or uncongenial conditions. Parenting, teaching, love, and cooperation depend for success on *following* nature or *amending* it.

The Greek philosophers of antiquity rightly distinguished "nature" from "convention" as different kinds of order. Much of human experience is purposive, and in this respect it differs from chemical reactions or the erosion of hillsides. Much of social science deals with the many ways human purposes are affected by natural phenomena, such as the human relations that make for (or undermine) effective work, teaching, or communication.

It has often been said, by thoughtful writers, that the social sciences have unique abilities to understand the motives and actions of fellow humans. The relevant idea is *Verstehen*, or "interpretive understanding." We can indeed describe—and not without confidence—the routine motives and behaviors of people we rely on and with whom we share everyday life. The proponents of *verstehen* were right to say that interpretation is an ever-present and indispensable component of human interaction. However, *verstehen* is at best a partial rendering of the postulate of humanity, which takes its departure from knowledge of human nature and the human condition, not from assumptions of mutual understanding. The postulate calls for empirical study of cultures and social worlds—that is, of the diverse ways in which minds are formed, incentives are generated, and norms of conduct established.

The study of juvenile gangs, military units, or indigenous communities requires something more than empathy. A common humanity is recognized, but what people have in common is not necessarily what we need to know. More problematic are special ways of cohesion and adaptation, which form and sustain distinctive states of consciousness. The evidence for those states may be intersubjective and in that sense "objective." But in social inquiry, *verstehen* plays only an ancillary part. We cannot depend on shared experience to describe and account for exotic forms of kinship, eating, or division of labor. Even if the main interest is in cultural uniformities, we need evidence that the asserted uniformity (with respect to religious symbolism or child-rearing practices, for example) is based on objective criteria.

"Methodological individualism" brings a postulate of humanity into philosophy and social science. The idea is that the "ultimate constituents of the social world are individual people who act more or less appropriately in the light of their understanding of their situation."[6] Methodological individualism does not question the reality of collective phenomena, such as group morale or collective decision. It does say that we can account for social configurations only when we find a global process to the attitudes or conduct of individual actors. The perspective appeals not to empathy but to the perceptions, evaluations, and feelings of individual persons responding to incentives or taking advantage of opportunities.

What we look for are phenomena that are recurrent but mostly undesigned. This is the framework within which purposes are pursued and institutions are built. Here "nature" and "convention" combine to create—often supporting and sometimes undoing—groups and norms.

Thus understood, naturalism is a spacious philosophy. Insofar as feasible, and with due attention to the stage of inquiry, we seek reliable indicators of what people think or feel, and how they relate to one another. These indicators may reveal inchoate or incipient change in collective life.

Naturalism does not dismiss or deprecate the expressive symbolism of religion, art, or politics; neither does it reduce religion to fantasy, politics to power, or love to attachment. Indeed, all reductionist strategies are suspect as failing to respect the integrity of the subject matter. Humanist naturalism is far removed from a cramped, self-limiting conception of empiricism. Instead it encourages a more open-minded and openhearted philosophy of nature. Naturalism takes ideals seriously and tries to describe and explain recurrent sources of frustration or aspiration.

Love and affection lead to mutual attraction and bonding. Those realities do not deny feelings or diminish obligations. So too, although science rejects supernatural beliefs, it need not ignore or negate the cultural and psychological contributions of religion or art. A political constitution allocates powers and duties, but it is also a framework within which animating ideals, such as equality and the rule of law, are made plain and protected. These manifestations of "spirit" are part of social reality, and as such are appropriate subjects for disciplined inquiry. This is the chief teaching of a spacious but science-minded naturalism.

3

Four Pillars of Humanist Science

WITHOUT A SPACIOUS NATURALISM, there can be no social science. We must be able to count, as part of nature, all the ideals and forms of thought, all the feelings and social arrangements that arise *without design* in the course of collective life. In every society we find principles of order, bonds of obligation, ardent symbolism, everyday rationality, and much else that marks a distinctively human existence.

A humanist naturalism, in affirming the postulate of humanity, asks of any social phenomenon how it affects the lives of people who live in the company of others, on whom they depend and from whom they need protection. Humanist naturalism rejects the view that there is an unbridgeable gap between fact and value. Instead it takes the interdependence of the two for granted and recognizes the continuity of what is subjectively desired and objectively desirable. What is desired varies in quality as well as in content. We need to know, and often can know, the rewards and frustrations—the promises and pitfalls—of personal and collective choice. We can discern latent ideals in nature, and learn what it takes to realize them.

Four mainstays, or pillars, of humanist science are (1) a concern for the quality of experience, (2) the interdependence of morality and well-being, (3) normative theory, and (4) the prevalence and efficacy of ideals or standards.

The Quality of Experience

Qualitative variation—in feeling, reasoning, perception, and relation—is a pervasive feature of human life. Differences in content—what people are taught, choose, do—are no challenge to the separation of fact and value. However, variations in quality are more problematic, in part because of the contribution they make to the enrichment or impoverishment of self-respect, self-scrutiny, and a readiness to desire what is truly desirable. We take account of qualitative variations when we recognize differences in skill, character, or initiative. For a humanist science, individual differences are less important than the shared experiences of work, education, religion, or politics. Here judgments must be made regarding qualitative differences in work, loyalty, prejudice, or deference to authority.

John Dewey gave special attention to the quality of experience. In his discussion of what it means to have "*an* experience," he emphasized the differences between routine and heightened consciousness, which he thought was a necessary part of the study of urgent needs or goals. Dewey connected these differences to aesthetic experience, which he associated not with art alone but with many kinds of "consummation." Some experiences are relatively superficial; others are compelling and memorable. Similarly, communication can be reserved or intimate, peremptory or negotiable, more or less well reasoned and respectful or humiliating, to be taken literally or with tacitly understood reservations. Much of social science has to do with such qualitative variations, notably in politics, management, and education. Consider also bonds based on trust and belonging. Bonding may be open-ended, or closely defined, as in many business transactions. How far the obligation reaches, and how much care it promises, are questions that go to the quality of the relationship.

Command and deference to authority are found in every society, and they are not necessarily demeaning or oppressive; they can emphasize desire or duty, be more comforting than painful and more uplifting than humiliating. It is not demeaning when a lower-court judge defers to the authority of a higher tribunal. Deference is acceptable when the reasons for subordination are readily grasped, for example when people at the scene of an accident obey the orders of police or firefighters. At issue is the quality of subordination—what it demands, how it is demarcated, what opportunities are offered for evasion or for redress of grievances.

In modern times, an important source of moral disarray is technological advance, especially techniques of persuasion and control. The benefits are not cost-free. Troubles stem from an "instrumental" logic, which treats people as readily deployable units or resources. New methods and incentives may intrude upon or disregard the organic unities of persons and groups. The Kantian injunction against treating people as "means only" is violated when evaluations are based on counting outputs or other narrowly defined criteria. Insofar as technology calls the tune, and a market mentality prevails, the postulate of humanity is disregarded, and a premise of intrinsic worth loses force.

The preceding discussion associates "quality" with "goodness." The connection is not forced or arbitrary, for it takes seriously the normative connotations of "quality." A "quality" product—fabric, book, performance—meets a high standard of production or expression.

Morality and Well-Being

A second pillar of humanist science is knowledge of what makes for the flourishing of persons, institutions, and practices. These ends require an understanding of what well-being means and how it is realized or distinguished. Morality calls for judgments about right and wrong, and those judgments speak to the character and integrity of a social unit. This conclusion rejects a radical separation of fact and value. The dualism is pernicious, as John Dewey said, in that it derogates the contribution of knowledge to moral judgment.

A pertinent strand of moral philosophy calls for fact-based assessment of consequences, and much is made of the difference between "consequentialist" and "deontological" judgments. Consequentialism holds that moral rules and actions should be judged by their effects on individual or collective conditions. In this view it has been said that it is morally wrong to cause unjustified suffering, to be wholly self-centered, or to undermine the values we associate with, say, teaching or healing. But well-being cannot be identified with "happiness" or "utility," unless those ideas are given very broad meanings, along the lines suggested by John Stuart Mill in the nineteenth century.[1] Consequentialists look to *desirable* conduct or policies, and what is desirable rests on something more objective than preference. We may prefer whiskey to fruit juice, but the preference is trumped by objective standards of health and self-control. Well-being entails the will to embrace and the knowledge to discern appropriate standards of vitality and good order.

In each approach, consequentialist or deontological, we appraise dispositions and outcomes, and we need to know what difference a course of conduct makes for the moral character of a person, practice, profession, or enterprise. Insofar as these effects are patterned or systemic, they can be described and explained by social science.

The study of effects or outcomes can also enhance a deontological ethic, insofar as it calls for following precepts as to what is right to say or do in the context at hand. Deontology is founded on commitment to a system or practice. We follow a deontological ethic when, for example, we uphold the moral equality of all persons. The warrant for the rule is a set of factual findings regarding harms or benefits. Thus understood, consequentialism and deontology are complementary ideas. Each considers outcomes, one for an order or agent, the other for external and desired conditions.

The meaning of "well-being" is obscured when we focus on short-run or narrowly defined gains or losses. Affluence and success bring many benefits, but their moral worth is not assured. Therefore, *self-scrutiny* is a moral imperative—to know what we prize, why we prize it, and what consequences our choices entail for a valued state of affairs. The focus is on *spiritual* well-being, which requires both self-scrutiny and self-transcendence. Spiritual well-being speaks to character and integrity, as when we assess the practices of an enterprise for how well or poorly it meets a standard. Spiritual well-being need not be single-minded. It takes account of competing values and pertinent contexts. Hence, *reflection* is a crucial aspect of moral judgment and a centerpiece of moral experience.

In Immanuel Kant's theory of morality, autonomy and rationality are necessary ingredients. A true child of the Enlightenment, Kant denied the moral worth of unexamined deference to tradition and received authority. That would be, in Kant's language, *heteronomy*, not *autonomy*.[2] Enlightened people rely on their capacity for reason; for them, rationality is an intrinsic part of autonomous judgment. Autonomy and rationality sustain an ethic of moral responsibility, the choice of duty over inclination, of the desirable over the desired. Kant's understanding of moral responsibility, however, gave insufficient weight to selfhood and authenticity. It was left to later generations to work out the existential and communitarian grounds of moral responsibility.

Post-Kantian thinkers sometimes ignored but did not sever the ties that bind reflection and responsibility. They argued that moral judgment is necessarily more local and prudential than a rationalist philosophy can allow. Shifting attention from *mind* to *self*, nineteenth-century thinkers saw selfhood as an attribute of institutions and communities, not only of persons. For them, moral reasoning is necessarily marked by internal dialogue and encounters with competing values.

Writers like Hegel and Marx thought history reveals a clash of opposites, and paths to reconciliation. They saw history as driven by contradictions and redeemed by cleansing conflicts. This "dialectical" approach uncovers the competing demands and recurrent dilemmas of moral experience.

The most important of these antinomies is that between *particularism* and *universalism*. Particularist obligations stem from kinship, ethnicity, friendship, and locality. These attachments form identities and thereby govern human lives. Particularism justifies preference for friends, relatives, and other in-group members. In contrast, an impersonal ethic detaches people from their special histories, making them subject to and beneficiaries of general criteria such as citizenship, residence, or merit. Divorced from social origins or connections, these more general criteria determine the distribution of burdens and benefits.

Although particularist and universalist principles are very different, people do not necessarily choose between them. Rather, both principles affect judgment and conduct, and this generates moral questions, such as who, if anyone, should be first in line for support or service. At the same time, moral principles are to some degree context-specific. What is appropriate in family life may be morally wrong in business or government. Families are sustained by particularist ideals, whereas a modern civil service or a professionally run business evokes more impersonal beliefs and policies. Different stresses, ambiguities, and calculations of costs and opportunities prevail.

The dilemmas are institutional as well as personal. Federal systems assign moral worth to constituent parts, such as local communities, because they are (or are thought to be) reliable centers of loyalty, initiative, and self-restraint.

A related source of moral unease was discussed by Max Weber in his essay on political and moral responsibility.[3] He explored the difference between an "ethic of conviction" (*Gesinnungsethik*) and an "ethic of responsibility" (*Verantwortungsethik*). The latter affirms obligations to particular persons, institutions, communities, or other going concerns. In contrast, an ethic of conviction prizes fidelity to abstract principles and is less likely to find compromise satisfactory. Weber's main point is that the "vocation of politics" should adhere to an ethic of responsibility and therefore should accept ambiguities and trade-offs. Yet Weber saw a place for the ethic of conviction as well. "At some point," he wrote, "fidelity to principle is a sign of moral responsibility." A true leader must be able to say, with Martin Luther, "Here I stand; here I remain; God help me, I can do no other." An ethic of conviction seeks purity of heart, freedom from self-reproach, and immunity from charges of betrayal and apostasy. An ethic of responsibility favors self-denial. Selfhood and integrity demand commitment to a common good, which can be realized only when competing interests are known and reconciled. When members have multiple commitments or face changing circumstances, purity of heart takes second place to the welfare of a particular family, church, party, agency, or nation.

These ideas point to a basic antinomy in moral experience: it is both *other*-regarding and *self*-regarding. It is other-regarding in that it demands respect and concern for the settings within which loyalties are formed and obligations are created and self-regarding in that the defense of a personal or social unit is also a defense of selfhood and identity. Morality is self-regarding insofar as it nurtures an ideal self and thereby sets standards and aspirations. Among these is self-respect, which is a foundation of trust and loyalty.

Normative Theory

The third pillar of humanist science is a commitment to theories that evaluate as well as describe or explain. This "normative" perspective is prevalent and even taken for granted in medicine, political science, economics, and social psychology. Each of these disciplines deals with problems that can be addressed only by positing or discovering what values, purposes, or ideals are in play. For example, political science examines the vicissitudes of constitutionalism and democracy; in economics, a key theme is the rationality or coherence of business enterprise; psychologists study mental health and pathologies as they affect emotional dispositions and effective communication. All these inquiries require evaluations of the state of a personal or social system. Evaluations are pursued while retaining fidelity to scientific standards of respect for facts. The premise is that a particular study can be "value-free" even as it addresses normative concerns.

Max Weber and "Value-Relevance"

Honored for his contributions to the sociology of religion, law, politics, and bureaucracy, Max Weber (1864–1920) added much authority to the ideal of "value-free" (*Wertfrei*) social science. He insisted on the separation of personal preferences from scholarly observation and reasoning. This dictum was needed, he thought, because some contemporary currents of thought encouraged scholars to express their own opinions.[4] Today this worry seems anachronistic. However, eliminating bias and wishful thinking—indeed, any unexamined preconception—is a well-established canon of responsible inquiry.

But Weber also believed that a "value-free" social science can and should have "value-relevance" (*Wertbeziehung*). In the study of religious, political, and other cultural phenomena, judgments must be made about, for example, "otherworldly" principles of legitimacy, which have subtle meanings and significant effects on economic, political, religious, and legal institutions. Speaking as a vigorous and self-conscious editor and scholar, Weber acknowledged that social scientists cannot forgo sensitive analysis of cultural phenomena. He insisted, however, that we can undertake that analysis without confusing our own likes or dislikes with what historical and comparative study may tell us.

Weber's thesis about value-relevance is now widely accepted. Contemporary social scientists are comfortable with studying the prevalence, variety, and remote effects of religious or political ideas, such as individualism, despite the evaluations they permit. Value-relevance, as Weber understood it, demands insight and subtlety but is quite compatible with the dualism of fact and value. Art, literature, and politics can be studied objectively, while also judging their human and moral significance.

Leo Strauss, a noted political theorist, wrote scornfully on this issue: "Would not one laugh out of court a man who claimed to have written a sociology of art but actually had written a sociology of trash . . . ? The prohibition of value judgments in social science would lead to the consequence that we are permitted to give a strictly factual account of overt observable acts in concentration camps; we would not be able to speak of these as cruelty. What would become of political science if we were not permitted to deal with narrow party spirit, boss rule, statesmanship, corruption, i.e. phenomena that are, as it were, constituted by value judgments?"[5]

As Strauss pointed out, when Weber actually analyzed religion, culture, and politics, he did not shrink from evaluations. "Weber had to choose between blindness to the phenomenon and value judgments. In his capacity as a practicing social scientist he chose wisely."

Ernest Nagel adopted a more conciliatory style when he distinguished two kinds of value judgment, which he called *characterizing* and *appraising*. The former is an evaluation of the degree to which some standard is approximated in a given instance, e.g., a biological indicator of disease. These value judgments do not necessarily entail approval or disapproval. Characterizing someone as a "good friend" says something about the relationship, without necessarily appraising it. The friend may be part of a criminal conspiracy. An appraising value judgment, on the other hand, is a conclusion that some envisaged or actual state of affairs is worthy of approval or disapproval. It is one thing to conclude on the basis of clinical tests that an organism is healthy or diseased; it is something else to welcome or deplore the fact. The clinical judgment is value-free in the sense that personal preferences are not relevant. Appraisal, on the other hand, brings inclination and purpose to bear.

When Strauss argued that Weber routinely made value judgments in the course of his studies, he had characterizing judgments in mind. Weber might have accepted Nagel's distinction, perhaps with some relief. The making of characterizing judgments is a necessary part of normative theory. In making these judgments, knowledge of qualitative states is sought, which are factual matters, to be interpreted with the aid of theories that depict a configuration or process.

The "Humanist" Marx

Karl Marx showed a "humanist" face in his critique of capitalism. He postulated a basic human nature—what he called "species nature"—which includes a striving for "free, conscious activity." He thought personal well-being depends on opportunities for autonomy, creativity, and responsible choice. This view, expressed by Marx in his theory of alienation, led to the conclusion that productive work is a positive good, not necessarily an evil or a burden.

The nineteenth-century factory system was, Marx thought, a breeder of alienation, that is, feelings of self-estrangement and oppression. Here, Marx spoke to the nature of human personality and the dehumanizing effects of capitalist industry. Many later writings on human relations in industry have come to similar conclusions: people suffer and morale is low when supervision is too close or when management is indifferent to human needs.

At the threshold of humanist science are two ideas: *morality* and *humanity*. Morality is a descriptive idea insofar as it refers to a condition or course of conduct governed by standards of good order and spiritual well-being. To understand this condition we must know what *restraints* societies impose as well as what *connections* they prize and protect. In every society lives are regulated; some form of authority is recognized; rules of deference are upheld. The lesson is that morality arises from ways of relating to others and their communities.

The centrality of normative theory does not preclude *non*-normative inquiry. In studies of voting, immigration, education, and much else, the main issues are not necessarily normative. They need not show bias or preconceptions. Study can be value-free, which contributes to a normative theory of self-democracy or adjudication. Research on a population's age distribution or sex ratio, or political attitudes and choices, or juvenile delinquency, or corporate governance, for example, could be value-free. The study may adhere to scientific standards, and qualitative assessments can be offered or expected. Such studies have scientific worth, but they are not distinctively humanist. Humanist social science looks beyond voting patterns to the quality of political decisions. Although the studies are empirical, they raise normative questions that are apparent when a community turns to social science for policy guidance. In a humanist science, normative questions are taken seriously, and their significance for personal and social well-being is explored. Normative concerns *affect* but do not *determine* the conclusions of empirical research. Humanist science is therefore not properly counterposed to empirical inquiry. Normative theory advances humanist concerns, especially values realized or at risk.

Ideals in Nature

The spacious naturalism to which I earlier referred extends to the study of all organic, need-reducing, problem-solving unities that emerge in society without conscious design or planning. An example is kinship, which demands loyalty and offers identity. The patterns are natural, in that they come about in response to recurrent urgencies and limited options. The institutions that we *design*, insofar as they are successful, take these undesigned conditions into account and try to make use of them, thus being able to plan "realistically." Studying nature, thus understood, serves human purposes. We learn what can be relied on and what must be guarded against.

Naturalism is by no means indifferent to ideals and does not dismiss them as unreal or ephemeral. Rather, ideals and standards are seen as founded on and sustained by the problem-solving efforts of human animals, whose social worlds make demands and evoke desires. Ideals found in parenting, teaching, judging, and craftsmanship are not arbitrary, nor are they expressions of raw preference. They are not brought on wings of angels or as Promethean fire. Standards arise from the failures that plague and the fulfillments that enrich human activities.

This understanding of ideals in nature is a prominent theme in Dewey's humanist naturalism. At one point he wrote that naturalism "finds the values in question, the worth and dignity of men and women, founded in human nature itself, in the connections, actual and potential, of human beings with one another and in their natural social relationships."[6] The same note was struck by George Santayana, who found clues to excellence in the urgencies of organic life.[7] For these philosophers, the idea of man in nature is a right image.

Seen in this light, morality has natural origins and natural uses. Caring, trust, good faith, and self-restraint arise from the snares and redemptions of social life. All societies discourage neglect of duty, and all demand obedience to lawful authority. The commandments may be clothed in vestments of divinity, itself a potent instrument of social control. Doctrines of revelation tell us something about the uses of symbolism, but they do not challenge naturalist explanations of obedience and reverence. A naturalist explanation does not, however, ease the anguish or diminish the complexity of personal choice. Untended gardens and neglected children have many causes, including youthful parents and tempting options. The options do not change what good gardening or good child care requires.

In a moral order, the leitmotif is responsibility. Every human purpose can be conduct that fails to meet appropriate standards of work or kinship. Each setting generates expectations of self-restraint and solidarity;

each has its own way of encouraging a transition from immediate gratification to enduring satisfaction. The standards are not necessarily noble or high-minded—they may describe a skilled burglar or assassin—nor are they self-justifying. They are judged by their success and by the postulate of humanity—that is, by universal or cosmopolitan ideals of obligation and care.

A naturalist account of human ideals accords with evolutionary theories of cognition, valuation, and development. "Fitness" and "adaptation" are key ideas. What matters is how well an organism or practice meets the demands and responds to opportunities. There are standards of success and failure, relative to competitors: better vision, coordination, strength, fertility—whatever confers an advantage for survival and reproduction. Outcomes are determined by objective conditions of health and competence. Implicit standards become explicit ideals as they are reworked by culture, a process that builds upon, and does not negate, the objective worth of health, courage, intelligence, and self-respect. Many different (and sometimes incompatible) goods are objectively good, and choosing one may foreclose the pursuit of others. Therefore a burden of choice remains, bringing with it responsibility for reflection and evaluation.

Finding ideals in nature does not preclude choice or judgment. A natural disposition (toward rage, for example) is not judged good just because it is "natural." We expect societies to promote or restrain natural tendencies, depending on whether they enhance or damage well-being, advance or retard the transition from immediate gratification to a deeper and more lasting satisfaction. A great aim of social science is to distinguish connections that create beneficial outcomes from mainly self-interested or self-indulgent wants.

Ideals are variably effective as spurs to constructive effort. Their best warrant and surest support are derived from an ensemble of dispositions, capacities, and arrangements that make human lives more cooperative, caring, and self-transcendent. The product is a human person more fully realized as a moral being.

Part Two   Realms of Value

4

From Social Order to Moral Order

WHEN DOES *order* become *good* order? When does *good* order become *moral* order? These are among the most challenging questions in moral philosophy and social theory. For answers we must examine the circumstances of choice and the imperatives of association. In doing so we transcend contexts and bring to bear more general principles of reason and morality, including what I have called the postulate of humanity.

The Moral Minimum

In the seventeenth century Thomas Hobbes propounded a famously "realist" theory of social order. He portrayed human life in its natural condition—in the "state of nature"—as "solitary, poor, nasty, brutish and short." Without sovereign authority, human lives are troubled by an unceasing quest for power and protection. The sorry outcome is a war of each against all—*bellum omnium contra omnes*. This unwanted and ungoverned condition is marked by disorder, aggression, and fear. The Hobbesian vision of self-preservation under conditions of anarchy and stress has a remedy: a "social contract" that restrains the worst forms of uncertainty and conflict by common assent to a sovereign authority, empowered to make rules and settle disputes.

According to this Hobbesian argument, order is a foundation of freedom, and this principle guides the design of political constitutions. This was well understood by James Madison and other founders of the American republic. Up to a point, we must all be Hobbesians. Nevertheless, taken by itself, the Hobbesian theory is myopic and misleading. It gives short shrift to the moral promise of political association, cannot deal with the full range of political concerns, and, above all, does not tell us how *social* order becomes *moral* order.

Hobbes was right to think of "order" as a chief concern. Every society must curb strife, limit crime, uphold authority, and defend the rightful expectations of ordinary people. Furthermore, many situations call for clear authority and ready obedience—for example, controlling unruly crowds. In many situations, however, order cannot be simply imposed. To secure conformity, something more than "command and control" is needed. Willing and informed obedience is the product of effective communication, and it presumes respect and self-restraint. In short, a more complex and quality-sensitive model is needed. The Hobbesian theory does not take account of these matters, nor does it deal with the needs of special contexts such as teaching or adjudication. Without studying such contexts, we cannot know what problems are created and what necessities or conditions lead to desired benefits.

The idea of a moral minimum is readily apparent in the criminal law, especially the "core crimes" of assault, murder, burglary, and robbery. Religious and secular institutions combine to uphold the peaceable conduct of ordinary lives. Rules become part of a taken-for-granted moral order, whose authority may be enhanced by appeals to divinity, as in the Mosaic Code. Such a moral order may remain rudimentary and precarious, marred by attitudes of revenge and retribution.

From Safety to Civility to Fellowship

The Hobbesian model guarantees safety for persons and possessions, yet it gives insufficient weight to shared understandings and patterns of self-help. In the moral order of a frontier community, where government is weak, people find security in their own resources, such as the support of kin and public indignation. Hobbes rightly claimed that a sheriff is needed to restrain violence and protect the defenseless. However, other contributions of the community through education and self-regulation are neglected. Insofar as the sheriff is an accountable officer of the law, he is held to standards that mitigate brutality and arbitrary action—for example, by protecting offenders from vigilante justice. In short, moral order emerges when the community and its institutions become sensitive to the interdependence of means and ends.

A Hobbesian remedy—sovereign authority—is only partly right. As problems arise that complicate the search for order, other values and interests are brought to bear. In a law-governed system, regulation of official violence is a major issue. In the law of war, an occupying power may impose a baseline morality to quell disorder. But raw domination is tempered by an ethos of moral and social responsibility, which is needed if the occupiers are to win the acquiescence and help they need. It is sound policy to encourage a transition from grudging conformity to willing cooperation, from bare-bones order to more robust signs of cooperation and restraint.

An ideal of civility emerges. Civility adds respect to restraint, thereby bringing new standards into play that have positive benefits for law enforcement and mark the transformation of absolute sovereignty into law-aiding government. Like other key ideas in moral and social theory, civility has both narrow and broad connotations. Narrowly understood, civility calls for external signs of deference, such as giving way or queuing up. A broader conception calls for respect as well as obedience. Beyond "taking turns" is a more demanding norm of "really listening" and trying to understand what someone else is saying. This deepened civility transforms arm's-length interaction into more active cooperation.

The need for security produces an elementary morality of restraint. This is a beginning, not an end. It must be supplemented by expressions of recognition and acknowledgment. Such norms are grounded in safety, but they reach beyond safety. They are building blocks of moral order. The Hobbesian model is a starting point, or perhaps a sketch of just and lawful authority. It is most relevant when elementary order is disrupted and when a more sensitive and multifaceted achievement is present. Hobbes offers a fruitful theory of the political foundations, not a developed social architecture.

The transition from safety to civility to fellowship marks a kind of moral evolution. Yet no such process is inexorable. The outcomes depend on many highly variable circumstances, which can be described but not foretold. In modern social science, many efforts have been made to trace patterns of moral evolution. A nineteenth-century example is Emile Durkheim's *Division of Labor in Society*, which describes the transition from "mechanical" to "organic" solidarity. The former finds social cohesion in likeness and conformity, whereas the latter arises from interdependence, reciprocity, and cooperation. Mechanical solidarity limits autonomy; organic solidarity assumes diversity of interests and outlooks. Similar ideas are found in research on child development, organizations, and political authority.

As these studies show, "development" is latent in and supported by emergent patterns of relatedness and consciousness. Although counterforces must always be expected, the *direction* is set by an unceasing quest for security and satisfaction. In Durkheim's model, self-interest mediates and advances the movement from mechanical to organic solidarity.

Consensus about morality offers indispensable clues to the practical worth of moral ordering.[1] Spurred by the social invention that we call contract, self-interest becomes a reliable basis for moral development. This is, however, a starting mechanism, not a fulfillment.

We should take seriously here the difference between necessary and sufficient conditions. Security is *necessary* for moral ordering but not sufficient. It must be supplemented by attitudes and practices of caring and respect. Elementary discipline and deferred gratification are then enhanced and transformed. At issue is the *kind* of security or discipline, not its elementary forms.

Since at least the seventeenth century, a state-centered system of deference and obligation has dominated public affairs. Although sovereign nations have been recognized as masters of their internal affairs, they are subject to treaties they have made and to customs they share. A nation's right to be, for example, a monarchy, democracy, or theocracy is accepted, but the right to engage in aggression or terrorism is not. At present, in international relations, the moral ideal is *comity*, not *community*. Comity says a nation-state should be free to define its own interests and wage war to protect those interests. The central value of comity is respect and a premise of civility.

In the twentieth century, the international moral order acquired new dimensions. Although sovereignty is mainly a political principle, its luster has dimmed. New forms of international organization have been created, together with new ways of thinking about the responsibilities of nations: the United Nations sponsors covenants against military aggression and nuclear proliferation, as well as agreements for the protection of human rights.

A panoply of nongovernmental organizations also pursues humanitarian goals and aids in the work of nation building. These developments have diminished the appeal of national sovereignty, presuming that the interests of humanity transcend the claims of nations. Such claims are by no means stilled, but national sovereignty has lost much of its hold on the political and legal imagination, trumped by calls for responsible participation in an international moral order.

Rights as Warrants of Moral Ordering

Like divinity, reciprocity, authority, and kinship, the idea of rights is a human invention. Every society allocates an array of rights to govern conduct. Rights add a moral dimension to customary or merely useful rules.

The emergence of a moral order is signaled by what Hannah Arendt called "the right to have rights."[2] Repelled by the aftermath of World War II, with its millions of displaced or stateless people, Arendt argued that the right to have rights presumes a civic identity, that is, belonging to a particular political community. She endorsed Edmund Burke's critique of "the rights of man," as set forth in his essay castigating the French Revolution. Burke claimed that rights should be understood as historical legacies, as when we speak of "the rights of Englishmen." Though Burke made a compelling case for connecting rights to historical contexts, he was wrong to slight cosmopolitan and universalist norms; he found no justification for rights that transcend the privileges of membership, such as rights against murder or torture.

Universalist rights do not require membership in a particular community, nor can they be dismissed as abstract or merely formal. They are rights sustained by sympathetic responses to suffering and deprivation—an attitude captured by the Christian doctrine of "neighborly love." The views of Burke and Arendt are insufficiently sensitive to human impulses for outreach and inclusion. The "right to have rights" is an expression of humanity, not of history, of fellow-feeling, not of parochial privilege.

This argument does not deny that rights are most secure when they are rooted in and acknowledged by particular groups or traditions. However, such traditions are not self-justifying; they rest on shared understandings of what humans want or need. This perspective helps create a moral order protecting universal entitlements at least to safety and respect. Each right or entitlement has rudimentary forms, and each may be elaborated to enlarge the obligations that people owe one another.

Rights, Contexts, and Social Inquiry

To identify and protect human rights we must know what aspects of human nature and the human condition affect personal and communal well-being. Social science studies rights in context, determining what rights are appropriate in the particular circumstances and how they may be implemented or restricted. These inquiries reveal the inner workings of business, government, or marriage. Each context has special features, which require (and make possible) different ways of giving effect to generic ideals of fairness. Some contexts require meticulous adherence to rules, while others permit more relaxed judgments. When the stakes are low, as in a traffic court, procedure can be rough. More careful adherence to procedural norms is required when heavy punishment is a prospect, for example in criminal courts.

Discovering the interests of all who may be affected is more important in an administrative or legislative inquiry than it is in an ordinary lawsuit. This difference calls for close study of how a system works and what interests are protected or in jeopardy. We benefit from analyzing the meanings and implications of "fairness," "discretion," and "arbitrariness," but there is no substitute for factual knowledge of what the context demands and what opportunities it affords.

This understanding of "rights in contexts" reminds us that a moral order is a *particular ensemble* of rules and principles. Expectations and choices are judged in the light of this concreteness, yet they do not preclude more general claims of right. Fairness, equality, and duty remain as critical principles for assessing the realities of government, employee relations, education, or parental love. An appreciation of contexts does not challenge philosophers or other theorists.

Rights and Moral Responsibility

As elements and warrants of moral ordering, rights are not divorced from responsibilities. Rights are asserted responsibly when doing so is mindful of consequences for others, and for the settings that people care about. It is morally wrong to insist on rights without regard to what that insistence may do to a marriage, a friendship, or a business. We should not equate *rights-centeredness* with the responsible assertion of rights. Rights-centeredness may invoke moral principles or be an expression of narrow self-interest. To assert rights responsibly is to think and act within a regulating matrix of norms and obligations.

In a functioning order, the recognition of rights is a beginning, not an end. Questions remain about their reach and justification, and their place within a larger framework of moral ideals. Rights may be acknowledged in narrow or merely formal ways, and their moral worth varies from one context to another.

A troubling temptation—the appeal to absolutes—affects the moral worth of rights. They are then thought of as unqualified trumps. If I have a right, it should not be limited by considerations of utility or the common good: a right to free speech is a right to say whatever I please regardless of consequences; a right to private property is a right to sell, destroy, or pollute what I own. In fact, however, the moral worth of a right depends on to what extent its assertion takes account of other concerns, such as a community's interest in safety or the environment. The assertion and acknowledgment of rights requires knowing what rights are at issue, how they should be asserted, and what the context allows and demands.

A first step identifies *kinds* of rights. Contractual rights may be closely specified, readily created, and as readily extinguished; other rights are indicators of good practice, as when we say that workers are entitled to occupational safety or to the orderly redress of grievances. The source of the right is not necessarily an agreement; it may be found, instead, in tacit promises. Rights are often created by experiences brought to bear from scrutinizing the language of a contract or statute. Here again, a "right to have rights" signals the existence of a moral order.

Solidarity and Respect

As warrants of moral ordering, rights signify a union of solidarity and respect. It is this that transforms a bare-bones social unit, held together by some practical dependency or by coercive domination, into one that affirms the worth and integrity of its parts. The parts may be individuals, families, localities, or units within a bureaucracy. All have claims to autonomy and enjoy rights of self-determination and consultation. They are not passive recipients of instruction or command and are not deployable or extinguishable at will. Instead, they are responsible agents and objects of moral concern. They are, in short, valued participants in a moral order.

A union of solidarity and respect is found in a great variety of groups that seek cohesion and effectiveness. The units of a bureaucracy have distinct identities and exercise autonomous judgment. In a well-ordered system of governance, officials owe duties to their special missions and the standards that those missions implement or defend. Such obligations are often incompatible with wholly centralized control. Responsible leaders pay that price as an acceptable cost of local initiative and commitment.

In 1788, the founding fathers of the United States expressed satisfaction that the new government would embody "the federal principle."

James Madison envisioned a political community founded on respect for the smaller unities. This principle was fortified by the related ideas of "covenant," "subsidiarity,"[3] and "pluralism," all of which postulate that social groups gain moral worth and greater unity when solidarity is grounded in an ethos of respect and forbearance. Bonds of solidarity are fashioned without surrendering local interests. Localities reserve to themselves rights and powers not explicitly granted to the center.

The federal principle is a far cry from the Hobbesian doctrine that autonomous groups are "lesser commonwealths within the bowels of the greater, like worms in the entrails of a natural man."[4] The pluralist ideal envisions limited centralization and a benign disorder. The individuality of groups and the uniqueness of persons are recognized, and diversity is welcomed as signifying the intrinsic worth of persons and groups, which are, for the most part, entitled to respect, not indifference or contempt. The federal principle envisions a more loosely coupled union. Concern for the worth and variety of social interests has informed most versions of pluralist thought, notably those that give full weight to the multifarious activities and relationships by which people advance their purposes and enrich their lives. "Civil society" refers to all these forms of cooperation and contention emerging from ownership, kinship, residence, and economic enterprises, as well as from religious, professional, and political affiliations. They take shape, for the most part, free of central initiative or direction, in the course of trading, spending, mating, working, and believing. The outcome is an intricate mosaic, whose protection and regulation are chief functions of the political community. The social reality that we call civil society is founded on pluralist doctrine, with its focus on local sources of energy and leadership. In this model the voices of "special interests" are governed but not stilled.

The federal principle and its pluralist cousins do not, however, justify fragmentation. It is a premise of pluralist doctrine that unity can be won while allowing for much independence and diversity. A federal constitution creates a limited central government, and an array of rights and powers is reserved to local or constituent parts. A pluralist order, like any social order, enforces standards of right conduct, which both allow and govern the freedoms of civil society: contract, association, reproduction, expression, and belief. Pluralism is not an enemy of order. It is a *kind* of order, which envisions a union of solidarity and respect.

Webs of Trust and Obligation

A moral order is largely composed of relationships based on trust and obligation. Interdependent people rely on one another with taken-for-granted assumptions about rights and responsibilities. Here moral theory and social science meet and interact.

An example is the difference between open-ended obligations and those that are conditional. The most familiar open-ended obligations are kinship and ethnic, national, religious, and institutional affiliations. The mutual obligations of parents and children are not closely specified. Rather, they are defined by unfolding circumstances. A valued person or group—whose needs and prospects are subject to change—cannot know in advance what its obligations may be. The prototype is a Western-style marriage: bride and groom accept one another "for richer or poorer, in sickness and in health."

Kinship and marriage are by no means the only sites of open-ended-ness. Friends, fellow citizens, coreligionists, and members of many associations accept similar commitments. Obligations run to those who share a commitment or belong to a community that is valued as a source of identity and belonging. Despite open-endedness, commitment is rarely truly unlimited. Loyalty may not be really unqualified. Moral theory helps us to understand the values at stake, but we also learn from experience what kinds of commitment a particular context requires. Patriotism appeals to feelings of belonging and self-transcendence. Yet it may be qualified by other values. These ideas may be articles of faith, with sacrifices freely made. The commitment is, however, not necessarily unconditional. In fact, it is contingent, variable, and context-sensitive.

Most obligations are *not* fully open-ended. Many are highly situational, even fleeting. The promises we accept, and benefit from, are blends of commitment and choice. Our most important choices create bonds that affect *future* choices. This interplay of choice and commitment is a vital aspect of marriage and many other relationships. In modern marriage, choice is decisive at the outset, but over time it diminishes in salience as a guide to decision.

Much the same may be said of employment, political affiliation, and professional associations. Choice is a background condition manifested in preferences expressed or implied in options for obedience or dissent, in low or high morale, or in separation and divorce. Webs of trust and obligation carry messages of responsibility that recognize and uphold the obligations. A thickening of relationships—to a friend, spouse, employee, or enterprise—is the substance of everyday moral obligation. Relationships reinforced by commitment, and by a deepened sense of responsibility, create more focused and demanding connections.

Ideals and Their Realization

In chapter 1 I referred to the centrality of ideals in the humanist thought of ancient Greece. This theme recurs in the modern science of moral ordering, which examines the governance of conduct by ideal standards. At issue is the *form* or *logic* of moral judgment, not its content or substance.

We should distinguish "ideals" from "values." Many experiences are prized for the satisfactions they bring. Preferences are taken as given, without scrutiny. However, when the *quality* of something prized is considered—a marriage, friendship, job, or political allegiance—we look to something more than a satisfactory state of affairs. An experience may be acceptable without being ideal. We bind values to ideals by attending to the quality of experience, thus revealing standards for criticizing the experience and assessing its moral worth.

Contexts and Latency

The study of ideals should consider the distinctive problems and purposes of a relationship or practice. Carpentry, education, science, lovemaking, parenting—each has standards drawn from experiences of success and failure, satisfaction and frustration. Standards are *latent* insofar as they arise from the activities of thinking, relating, or helping.

Fidelity to context is a necessary maxim, but it should not neglect the ideals that transcend context. Purposes and settings are not necessarily unique. They fall within broader categories and may be governed by more comprehensive ideals, such as nurture, deliberation, or fairness. These master ideals identify what standards are relevant in the context at hand. Thus deliberation takes many forms, for ideals of truth finding and integrity transcend particular contexts. What deliberation means and how it promotes fidelity to context are issues that require thoughtful study. Although fidelity to context recognizes special constraints and opportunities, it does so without losing sight of a governing ideal. The ideal is necessarily general, often elusive, often contested. General principles are useful guides to appropriate, context-sensitive decisions, such as what constitutes fairness in the exercise of parental authority. That the ideals are elusive and hard to identify is challenging but not necessarily disabling.

Empirical Issues

The idea that general principles are necessary for and consistent with fidelity to context is a salute to moral philosophy. We cannot do without the illumination gained from philosophical analysis of fundamental ideas.

In a science of moral ordering the chief concerns are (1) to identify distinctive or animating ideals and (2) to learn what conditions affect their realization. We need to know what constitutes successful effort in a particular sphere of life, such as education or gardening. Each sphere has ideals of right conduct, which are not easy to spell out; nor is it obvious what troubles or opportunities will be encountered. Here Lon Fuller's concept of "internal morality" is helpful.[5] A student of jurisprudence, Fuller was mainly concerned with the "internal morality" of adjudication, legislation, and mediation. His idea has a broader significance, however, extending to any form of cooperation governed by distinctive criteria of success: in family life, highway engineering, or military training, for example. The internal morality is revealed by a theory that tells us what ends are appropriate and what means are effective. This is not a purely analytical exercise. It requires empirical data regarding what works well or is, instead, a disabling source of distortion or frustration.

Any ideal is subject to attenuation, debasement, or incomplete re-alization in some other way. Some ideals are especially precarious, that is, highly susceptible to distortion or attenuation, when values are vul-nerable or made precarious by special pressures and temptations. It is sometimes said, with much justification, that ideals are *necessarily* incom-pletely realized. Indeed, every ideal is a judgment on what is actually accomplished, since ideals are abstract, whereas experience is concrete. Ideals of friendship, responsibility, and self-government may never be completely realized; but the ideal is approximated more closely under some conditions than others.

A persistent question remains: Is the ideal attainable? Or is it *uto-pian*? A utopian ideal lacks practical efficacy and is unable to deal with real-world problems without loss of moral worth. For some political theorists, notably Robert Michels and Gaetano Mosca, "democracy" and "equality" are mere "political formulae," which can influence political reality but can never be made good: The egalitarians might win, they say, but not equality; "the socialists might win, but not socialism."[6] In this view, the banners of idealism are screens behind which struggles for power take place. These "realist" theories offer valuable insights and are useful as *cautions*, but they do not acknowledge (or study) the many ways in which ideals inform moral judgment and social policy. *Pure* democ-racy and *complete* equality may well be unrealizable, but those ideals are relevant insofar as they guide institutional design and insofar as they offer principles of criticism and visions of reform. If the ills and deficiencies of democracy are faced, appropriate safeguards can be instituted; equality can be furthered by overcoming invidious discrimination, enlarging op-portunity, and extending legal protections. Such policies are "realistic" in that they take account of limiting and countervailing circumstances, and they respond to historical opportunities by correcting deficiencies and criticizing shortsightedness.

Critics of idealism have too often accepted an all-or-nothing approach. This is a flight from realistic *design*. The fate of ideals is determined by their prospects for survival in uncongenial settings: this was Alexis de Tocqueville's thesis when he traced the impact of an egalitarian ethos on the institutions of modernity. Ideals of art, learning, and democracy are not necessarily lost or killed. They may, however, be harmed or distorted, as when an ideal of self-government is equated with rule by referendum or willing submission to a demagogic leader.

These are questions for a social science marked by concern for relevant values. The variable realization of ideals suggests a need for inquiry into the ways in which purposes are narrowed or enlarged, displaced, undermined, or only partly achieved. In subsequent chapters, I examine recurrent sources of vitality and decay. In this way, I propose an agenda for a humanist science of social life.

5

Humanist Virtues

THE INTERPLAY of ideals and realities is especially evident in the study of virtues, which are best understood as *states*—dispositions, competences, forms of organization—subject to variation and assessed in light of how they help or hinder desired outcomes. A science of virtue, like all science, is theoretical as well as empirical: theoretical in that it posits a personal or institutional "nature" and empirical in that its elements react to envisioning influences. This variability calls for factual and descriptive accuracy, yet is normative as well as descriptive. A person or institutional "nature" includes vulnerabilities and resiliencies. Empirical study examines these conditions and therefore assesses the system's moral competence. A humanist science treats moral competence as variable, sustained by some actions and diminished by others.

Persons and Institutions

Persons and institutions are very different in some ways, notably in specific dispositions and impulses. They are similar, however, in the capacities they create and the functions they serve. Organizations have *memories* and *identities*, sustained by trained professional staffs and by established procedures. The outcome is a distinctive unity or character.

Institutional memories are not personal, but their functions contribute to the competence and direction of the institution. In business, reliable suppliers, customers, and marketing specialists are recognized.

These reflections suggest that the study of virtues is institutional as well as personal. Responsiveness, rationality, independence, and fidelity to purpose are sustained by supervision and informal education. Personal and institutional virtues have closely similar functions and require analogous resources of reflection and control.

Socialization for Ideals

In a humanist science of virtue, practices are scrutinized for the harms or benefits they bring; and for the light they cast on the postulate of humanity. In this chapter I examine the social and psychological bases of moral well-being. A key process is "socialization," which transforms human animals into effective participants in a moral order. Shared ideals of respect and obligation are developed and transmitted. Socialization occurs in all groups, and each has its own conception of the well-formed person: an understanding of what may be expected and required. Every society—and every enduring group—wants and needs members with appropriate skills and values. In Western society, the well-socialized person respects ideals of freedom, honor, responsibility, dignity, rationality, and authenticity.

Individuality and Freedom

Being a "person" is a condition marked by *presumptive* capacities, obligations, and rights. To be recognized as a person is to be treated as belonging, first, to the community that includes all humanity. This generic personhood is distinguished from the special identities of residence, ethnicity, or occupation. The United States Constitution guarantees to every "person," citizen or alien, due process of law and equal protection of the laws. In the controversy over abortion, for example, the chief question is whether a fetus is a "person" in contemplation of law, entitled as such to legal recognition and protection.

"Person" connotes a condition we call individuality and an entitle-ment we call freedom. Individuality stems from the particularity of human existence, including the special ties people have to other persons, ideas, and groups. Such connections are prime sources of nurture and status.

The disposition to personalize what we value accounts for much religious symbolism. In the pantheon of ancient Greece, the gods are much involved in human affairs. Though perceived as immortal, they were thought to share many human traits such as jealousy, sympathy, or anger. Christians venerate God the Father, stern but just; a divine and nurturing Mother; a loving and self-sacrificing Son.

The individuality of persons is not well grasped by the ideology of "individualism," which relies on abstract categories and judgments. In that perspective, people are "abstract" individuals defined by categories that transcend or ignore differences of history and affiliation. Abstract indi-viduals are fungible units of effort, obligation, or entitlement: employees, soldiers, or citizens, rather than fully realized or described participants in social life. The hero of individualism is a contracting party whose rights and obligations are the same as those of anyone similarly situated. A prac-tice of favoring friends or relatives—nepotism—is a scandal, not a duty. The precepts of individualism uphold ideals of fairness, but do not speak to such moral issues as balancing the needs of systems and those of persons.

The person-centered philosophers of the nineteenth century, such as Herder and Hegel, resisted modern individualism. They argued that persons are historically determined, nurtured by particularity, indelibly marked by distinctive forms of attachment and self-expression. These ideas anticipated a more recent conception of persons as "embedded" in the supports, opportunities, and obligations of group life. Embed-dedness suggests wholeness and an illusion of self-determination. Self-determination is experienced as a kind of freedom. The relevant values are *integrity* and *self-respect*, including freedom to associate with kin-dred others and to respond as whole persons rather than as a rule may require or allow.

The connection between individuality and freedom is not remote. The main concern is *coherence*—that is, the persistence of a certain *kind* of person, practice, group, or institution, commitments that run to beliefs, to traditions, or to a special competence or relationship, such as being a wife and mother. The quest for coherence stems from a need for authenticity, the inner unity and well-being produced by feelings of commitment and identity.[1]

Personal freedom is wholly compatible with belonging and conformity. "To thine own self be true," says Hamlet's mentor. Polonius invokes an ideal of self-defining choice, and this may explain why "choice" has so much moral resonance today. Most choices have limited significance, but the opportunity to select from a range of options is highly prized.

In his justly celebrated essay *On Liberty*, John Stuart Mill saw individuality as the psychic and moral foundation of a libertarian philosophy. He argued that personal freedom is essential for human flourishing and is therefore a valid basis for resisting conformity. It is "the privilege and proper condition of a human being, arrived at in the maturity of his faculties, to see and interpret experience in his own way."[2] Mill believed in an individuality whose most urgent needs are freedoms of self-formation and self-expression. Democracy calls for *political* liberty, but human flourishing requires a more *personal* liberty.

Mill's perspective was prefigured in Karl Marx's early "humanist" writings. Marx thought it part of man's "species nature" to seek and enjoy "free, conscious activity." This premise led to humanist conclusions about work and authority. People need to work, Marx thought, but work should be constructive and self-fulfilling, without turning humans into appendages of machines.

Personal freedom is not unlimited, nor is it freedom of just any sort. It is the freedom of integrated selves to experience self-respect and the respect of others. Respect for individuality does not preclude conformity; rather, special ways and impulses are encouraged or allowed.

A related ideal underpins conscientious objection to military service. A plea to be excused from the draft is supported by a personal history of adherence to pacifist faiths. Despite a policy of shared sacrifice, government accepts the claims of persons who adhere to nonconformist beliefs.

Responsibility and Commitment

Among the salient virtues of persons is responsible conduct. An ethic of responsibility is not an arbitrary choice or a divine command; it is a product of connectedness and interdependence. Fully realized persons have identities based on kinship, ethnicity, religion, occupation, ideology, or locality. In these contexts, rights are entwined with duties, as when parental rights of possession and supervision are combined with duties of support and nurture.

Moral responsibility derives from the realities of belonging and identity. Responsibility and selfhood are connected, and this helps clarify the difference between being *accountable* and being *responsible*. Accountability has to do with obeying rules and achieving goals; successes are rewarded, failures punished. Responsibility is a more personal and open-ended standard. Responsible parents, employees, soldiers, or corporate leaders act in accord with what a situation demands, not only by following rules or obeying commands. Discernment, creativity, and knowledge of the reasons behind a rule are called for. When people act responsibly, external controls can be relaxed. Supervision is about empowerment, and participants are helped to make good judgments and contribute their best efforts. Responsible conduct is a kind of *stewardship* for the well-being of a person or project.

Many important commitments are subtle blends of particular loyalties and general principles. Marriage, friendship, parenting, and religious life are governed by implicit standards of achievement and behavior. Policy becomes less definite and more vulnerable because it is not wholly clear which obligations are truly binding and which are optional or subject to revision. Most responsibilities are limited, as are most obligations created by a typical contract. Others, such as those arising from marriage and procreation, are more comprehensive, enduring, and indefinite. The conflict between limited and open-ended obligations can often identify the social and moral significance of a role or relationship.

Moral ordering often requires a "federal" principle, whereby a larger unity is created that recognizes the integrity and intrinsic worth of the

constituent parts. The latter may be individual persons or relatively autonomous regions or groups. The "federal" order fosters respect for diversity as well as unity. Thus participation is *self-preserving*. Responsible
political participation takes place in and through other, often *nonpolitical*,
affiliations. In some demanding religious or political groups, for example,
the communicant is effectively detached from prior associations and becomes available for unconditional loyalty and sacrifice.

The United States Constitution, adopted in 1789, created a democratic republic, whose full nature remained unsettled and controversial.
Some matters, such as the need for a Bill of Rights, were rapidly settled;
others, such as issues having to do with the reach of centralized power,
were more difficult. The Jeffersonian Republicans thought the Union
was a compact among the several states, whose basic sovereignty was
reserved; therefore the states could "nullify" and refuse to obey selected
federal legislation. Their opponents, the Federalist Party, argued that the
phrase "we the people" should be understood as creating a strong national government. It took almost a century, and a civil war, to decide
these issues.

A frequent source of moral disquiet stems from the opposing claims
of piety and principle. In many situations, including family life, loyalty
runs to particular others with whom one's own life is connected. Piety
and authenticity enhance individual and social coherence. People gain
wholeness and continuity from affirmative attitudes toward their origins
and their most important bonds. They make choices within frameworks
of commitment and loyalty. Therefore choice by itself is not a clear or
untroubled part of morality.

This argument is not new. A number of nineteenth-century thinkers found moral worth in historical or cultural continuities. Denying
the claims of autonomy, they were drawn to a morality of piety, which
George Santayana called reverence and respect for "the sources of one's
being"[3]: family, schoolmates, coreligionists, fellow soldiers, fellow citizens. Yet these are emptied of significance when latent ideals are lost or
tarnished. Friendships are weakened and memories fade as people drift
apart and lose their hold on selfhood.

On Being Human

I said before, without elaboration, that being a "person" is a status we ascribe to all humans. Every person has a presumptive claim to individuality, as well as presumptive obligations of responsibility to others. These assumptions are grounded in shared understandings of human nature and in the pervasive realities of lives lived uneasily in groups and communities. These conditions establish what it means to be human and therefore what the postulate of humanity demands.

A Realm of Spirit

Human animals have impulses that they share with other species, notably the "tissue tensions" of hunger, thirst, and sex. In these and many other respects, human lives are not unique. However, humans do have special capacities for language, thought, and communication, for memory, myth, and art.

Language, more than a useful tool, is a prime resource for cultivating emotions, such as reverence, hostility, and solidarity. Language also encourages a quest for meaning, thereby creating a "realm of spirit." As Santayana said, this realm is grounded in the material conditions of everyday life but reaches beyond those foundations toward intellectual, religious, and aesthetic appreciation. That every human community creates a realm of spirit, thus understood, is a chief conclusion of social anthropology. For Franz Boas and other modern anthropologists, the "mind" of primitive man[4] is everywhere manifested in culturally defined modes of self-realization and expression. The human spirit takes many forms, but beyond those differences is a universal human nature, sometimes called the "psychic unity of mankind." The human spirit is vividly expressed in a common tendency to create valued ways of life within which identities are formed, reinforced, and passed down.

The most important component of the realm of spirit is the pursuit of ideals. Ideals are not extraordinary or exotic. They adorn and direct growth and maturation, and are supported by attitudes of approval or disdain. Mastery for excellence is everywhere a hallmark of social success.

Standards are necessary for much psychological and physical development: toilet training, learning to walk, clean up, work, hunt, fight, play, cooperate. Indeed, standards saturate experience in many contexts and at every age. Some ideals make only limited demands and are easily met. Others, more subtle or abstract, require much study and experience. Therefore spiritual life is fortified by special instruction and sacred or exemplary texts and rituals. The meanings of many ideals—love, integrity, self-government, justice—are far from self-evident. Therefore reflection and instruction are needed to encourage considered judgment and choice.

Irrepressible Conflicts

The virtues of persons are made plain by pervasive conflicts and dilemmas. Especially important is the reconciliation of abstraction and concreteness. Abstraction blurs and sometimes erases differences in merit or achievement. For example, equality as an abstract idea curbs privileges; however, it has moral costs, insofar as it dims awareness of particular histories and the special circumstances that may excuse unwelcome behavior or justify special help. In criminal cases, for example, abstract criteria of responsibility—such as a requisite intent—may determine guilt or innocence. The penalty, however, takes into account motives and capacities. One whose actions display an "abandoned heart" or "reckless disregard" of harm to others is likely to receive a harsher penalty. Judges are expected to adapt the legal conclusion to particular circumstances, which may call for a lighter or a harsher penalty.

Abstraction is the wholly legitimate (if sometimes wayward) child of principled classification. But reflection is concrete as well as abstract; it takes account of whole persons and treats them as having intrinsic worth. The conflict between abstract and concrete morality appears in the competing claims of "universalism" and "particularism." Universalism presumes a community committed to a general principle, whereas an ethos of particularism identifies members and excludes strangers. Universalism is reinforced by education and the rule of law, particularism by kinship and other special affiliations. A well-ordered community relies on both moralities. Norms of obligation encourage parents to help children go to school, while the schools make their own, more impersonal judgments. The particularism of family life is offset by universalist ideals of achievement and merit.

A related theme recognizes the fact that individuals are separate as well as interdependent. Separateness is often obscured by the claims of obedience and cooperation. Interdependence comes to the fore when social bonds are absent or break down, and people who are connected accept limits but do not give up their reserved rights as distinct individuals. Contemporary liberal philosophy has made much of separateness.[5] In an earlier, Hobbesian theory, the "state of nature"—a condition prior to the establishment of governing authority—is marked by a struggle of separate individuals and groups for protection and aggrandizement.

In the seventeenth century John Locke found, in his own conception of the state of nature, norms of cooperation, attachment, and accord. For Locke, people in the state of nature lack the "convenience" of political authority, but they do not lack moral will or resources. He found the main source of order and of rights in *society*, not *government*. In this view, government is a derivative institution whose legitimacy and efficacy depend on infrastructures of cooperation, loyalty, and respect. Locke took for granted that the separateness of persons would be protected by legitimate governments, for example by upholding rights in property, especially property in one's own person.[6] Locke's theory was not a prescription for surcease of struggle. He expected sustained effort to reconcile the conflict between individuals, who have ultimately separate interests, and the claims of collective action and the common good. Though Locke did much to foster an ethic of individualism, his real aim was to reconcile the separateness of individuals with the realities of interdependence and association. Separateness calls for protection of rights, whereas interdependence requires effective collective institutions.

Collusion of Good and Evil

The accommodation of separateness and association raises a number questions: What kind of self should people aspire to have? How open and engaged? How detached and uninvolved? The pragmatist philosopher

William James thought a blend of openness and engagement would signal inner strength and moral awareness. New situations should be approached with confidence, yet a spirit of reconciliation and fellowship should prevail, developing new strategies for broadening horizons. This affirmative option does not seek *elimination* of self; rather, it contemplates the construction of a self in communion with others.

The tension between openness and closure is not readily finessed. There is value in *individual* integrity, but not when it involves harm to other values and broader interests. Adam Smith wrote eloquently of the "invisible hand" that unites private gain and public benefit. However, this truth is limited and partial. Not less well recognized are the many ways in which the unregulated pursuit of self-interest leads to public costs, such as environmental damage or other market failures.

The collusion of good and evil is apparent in many proposals for social reform, since good intentions frequently have unintended effects. It is good to help people in distress, good to get rid of oppressive regimes. But the means used to achieve those ends often create unforeseen evils, such as demoralizing dependency or sacrifice of bystanders.

Selves and Persons

The preceding discussion has had two main subtexts: that selves are contingent products of social circumstances and that the quality of personhood significantly affects its virtues and vicissitudes. "Selfhood" is not a synonym for "personhood." Selfhood is a *component* and *condition* of personhood. The prime virtues of a fully realized person are integrity and moral competence, but good moral judgments are not made by people whose selves are weak or distracted. In psychological therapy or moral education, an effort is made to help people gain the self-knowledge and emotional stability they need to be autonomous *and* responsible. In uncongenial contexts, selves lose the capacity to sustain the virtues of persons.

This perspective invites inquiry into the formation of selves. Connections between psychological states and group life, especially between psychological states and the requirements of good order, are shown in psychological studies of maturation and regression. Sources of free-floating or uncontrolled aggression are considered, as are individual capacities for trust and cooperation. Healthy or unhealthy selfhood affects marriage, teaching, and much else. If children are neglected or abused, they have trouble feeling good about themselves, trusting others, and being trustworthy. The pathologies reveal how much personhood depends on selfhood, nurture, and support.

Master social trends can exacerbate the process of developing selfhood. Broad changes affect kinship, work, religion, and popular culture, creating a "representative" or "basic" personality, marked by strengths or weaknesses, widely shared anxieties, and attitudes of insularity or openness. Many such patterns have been noticed in modern history. Events in the sixteenth and seventeenth centuries, such as the Protestant Reformation with its assault on entrenched ecclesiastical authority, the rise of entrepreneurial capitalism, and, later, the French and American revolutions, projected a strong sense of self-confidence in human abilities, undaunted by received authority.

These occurrences opened minds and lifted spirits. They gave shape to the outlooks of businessmen, churchmen, politicians, philosophers, and artists. In time, however, other trends took hold, such as the breakdown of traditional, premodern ways of life, a trend accelerated by winds of doctrine that prized reason, equality, democracy, and moral pluralism. The outcome was a world made new, marked by pervasive uncertainty and "other-directed" thought. At the same time, for large populations the world seemed more opaque and out of control. These readings of modern history are not wholly convincing, but they suggest that widely shared social conditions significantly affect how people feel and think about others and themselves.

The study of selfhood and virtue is both conceptual and empirical. It seeks to clarify and elaborate ideas, by analyzing the logic of a perspective or outlook and thus opening the door to philosophical imagination and philosophical history. The union of philosophy and social science furthers historical, contextual, psychological, and institutional inquiry. There is no sharp boundary between the conceptual explorations of Max

Weber, Emile Durkheim, Alfred Marshall, George H. Mead, Chester I. Barnard, Friedrich Hayek, Talcott Parsons, and Robert K. Merton—all social scientists—and the writings of philosophers like Locke or Hume, whose work explored recurrent aspects of the social world. They were all ready to have their ideas judged by how well or poorly they accounted for events. They thought of themselves as scientists *and* philosophers.

According to the liberal tradition, notably in the writings of John Locke, legitimate government rests on "the consent of the governed." However, empirical study reveals *kinds* of consent, some beneficial, others harmful. Adolf Hitler sought consent for his regime, but he was happy to get the approval of a dubiously national plebiscite, unvexed by opposition or debate. The true ideal is *self-preserving* consent, not a raw expression of approval.

Similarly, in the study of socialization, we may distinguish "repressive" and "participatory" kinds. Repressive socialization relies on punishment, rejection, and top-down authority. Participatory socialization rests on willing cooperation and personal autonomy. Each kind expects conformity, but the psychological mechanisms and effects are very different, especially with respect to freedom and responsibility.

6

The Morality of Governance

AMONG THE SOCIAL SCIENCES, political science is especially open to normative concerns. This is true despite a resolutely non-normative "behaviorist" trend, which espouses a strict separation of fact and value. However, the pull of policy is strong, as is the connection between political science and political philosophy. Legitimacy, constitutionalism, representation, and civil liberty are lively topics, each pointing to values realized and at risk. In this chapter I discuss some themes that reflect the value-centered core of political inquiry.

Politics: "High" and "Low"

There is a persistent ambiguity in the way "politics" is understood in common speech as well as in scholarly inquiry. An implicit distinction between "high politics" and "low politics" is readily discerned. "Low politics" is another name for power politics—that is, for strategies that seek public support or the favor of officials. In contrast, "high politics" is controversy regarding principles affecting public welfare. Both forms coexist and sometimes reinforce one another; they are also often at odds.

Political partisans commonly use the idiom of high politics. As has been said of hypocrisy, this is the tribute that vice pays to virtue.

Partisan strife is tainted by self-seeking and a readiness to do "whatever it takes" to "climb the greasy pole."[1] Low politics readily lends itself to non-normative inquiry, but it will not reveal what virtues are lost or impaired when, for example, elections are rigged or officials are corrupted. Although low politics deserves its bad repute, there is, in fact, an interplay of low politics and high politics. The relevant questions are these: How does low politics enter into official decisions? How can the connection be regulated? These normative concerns can be addressed only by knowing what the context makes possible—that is, what we can aspire to and what we must guard against.

Responsive Government

In the twentieth century political scientists had much to say about the power of "interest groups." For some writers, the topic was mainly descriptive: how interest groups are formed; what their recurrent strategies and tactics are; how they influence politicians, journalists, and government officials. Normative issues cannot be avoided: Is the influence of interest groups mainly pernicious or are they legitimate voices that should be heard? A positive attitude toward interest groups underlies the ideal of *responsive* governance.

Responsiveness posits the moral and political worth of nongovernmental groups and activities. Decisions are "transparent," and a flourishing civil society is taken to be the infrastructure of good government. This principle is upheld when, for example, a government gives public notice of new rules and projects, such as the construction of a dam or highway. The government agency invites argument about costs and benefits. Responsiveness thereby strengthens participation and welcomes criticism.

Responsive government is prudent as well as transparent. A sound plan of interest-group representation takes into account costs as well as benefits. A potential downside of responsiveness is that it may respect some interests while neglecting others. A degenerated form of responsiveness is *opportunism*, which favors an interest chiefly because it is influential. The virtue of responsiveness considers what kinds of participation bring out facts and issues that might otherwise be overlooked.

To be responsive rather than opportunistic, public policy must be open in some ways and closed in others: open to new voices and horizons, but closed by concern for its self-defining values. An institution cannot be responsive if it fails to see (and therefore will not meet) new challenges or if it forgets or forsakes its core values and main purposes.

The burden of responsiveness is encountered in families, churches, business firms, and schools—wherever challenges are met by combining openness to new ways with received understandings of purpose and policy. Therefore responsiveness, like all moral ideals, demands self-scrutiny and self-knowledge.

The Paradox of Power

Power is indispensable as well as perilous, a steady source of ambiguity and trouble. In most enterprises and communities, some people control and others obey; little can be done without unequal distributions of influence and privilege. The inequalities are *necessary*, but not *innocent*. They pose a master problem for political science: how to keep the benefits of unequal power while curbing overreaching.

Responsiveness is improved by philosophical analysis of meanings and values—for example, how "authority" differs from "power" or which interests merit what kinds of acknowledgment. These questions evaluate as well as describe. Analysis is not enough. Hence, the realization or frustration of ideals requires empirical study of how people associate, cooperate, and compete.

As was noted earlier, we should identify kinds of authority and kinds of consent. These variables affect the distribution and protection of rights, which differ considerably in scope and salience. We readily distinguish "basic," "natural," or "constitutional" rights from others that can be more easily changed or extinguished, perhaps by revising a contract or by a legislative vote. In 1776 the American Declaration of Independence asserted that certain rights are fundamentally self-evident truths. "Among these rights," it said, are "life, liberty, and the pursuit of happiness." These unalienable or natural rights are vulnerable to Jeremy Bentham's caustic comment that they are "nonsense upon stilts."[2] Bentham spoke truly about most rights, which can be modified or negated by acts of will and by private or public agencies. Examples are rights of marriage, divorce, or procreation. Bentham, however, failed to distinguish *kinds* of rights. There are rights of parents to custody of their children, of prisoners to freedom from abuse, of dissenters to speak their minds. These and many other rights stem from convictions about individuality and personhood, or from conceptions of intrinsic worth. They limit what public officials can do for the sake of social benefits or "utility."

Moreover, important differences exist in the ways rights are asserted. Many claims of right have little moral significance, especially if they screen greed and self-seeking. Rights gain moral worth when they are asserted to vindicate a cause or principle that transcends self-interest.

The *classification* of rights is a kind of *assessment.* Criteria of evaluation are built into the classification. A theory may tell us what rights are needed for personal or collective well-being. The doctrine of "states' rights" in American constitutional discourse, for example, has rested on a theory of federalism.

The variety and contingency of rights were major themes in the perspective of Justice Louis D. Brandeis. He and his "realist" colleagues on the Supreme Court brought an empiricist outlook into a chamber long comfortable with ungrounded abstractions, arguing that jurisprudence must take account of practice as well as thought and advocating a keener sense of how the system works, with what effects. "The life of the law," said Justice Oliver Wendell Holmes, Jr., "is not logic but experience."[3] Holmes did not mean to disparage logical arguments or appropriate classification. Instead, he wanted to inform the work of the Court with knowledge of social purposes and machinery. An important contribution of legal realism was its conception of the common good. Something more was at stake than the critique of abstractions, more also than resistance to oracular utterance. At their best, the legal realists defined the public interest as emerging from a collective intelligence that responds to the realities of association, ownership, and conflict.

Earlier I said that in distinguishing low politics from high politics we should not ignore their *connection.* Debate about issues is in part a bid for attention and support; it is part of power politics. The civil-disobedience tactics of the civil rights movement of the 1960s showed this connection. A moral ideal of governance channels the politics of power into constructive forms of public discourse.

Beyond Diversity

A claim to the sovereignty of *will* is deeply offensive to moral awareness, which posits a fundamental source of criticism. *Thy* will be done, say religious believers. Morality invokes a transcendent truth—one that trumps the will of any human, however elevated, learned, or ignorant. This teaching runs counter to much of modern thought, which embraces the motto "man makes himself" and finds comfort in the plurality of cultures and the historicity of minds. There are indeed many ways of showing and deserving respect. However, the idea of a *common humanity* overrides differences in history and culture. All peoples are similar in vital respects even though they differ in conduct and belief.

A Hermeneutic Imperative

The diversity and complexity of human situations signals a need for interpretation, thus bringing a subjective element into the analysis of rules and principles. Variations in law, religion, and warfare offer many reminders that blunt commands are not to be taken as the last word. They are amended by principles that reveal implicit norms that modify rules and rework meanings. A working moral order is likely to produce designated interpreters of moral truth: priests, scholars, judges, shamans, prophets.

A familiar manifestation of transcendent moral authority is *constitutionalism*. A king, at his coronation, may swear "to uphold the laws of the realm," and a constitutional court has the last word, for the case at hand, as to what the constitution means. Judgments are subject to further thought by different judges, and may find authority in other interpretations on different subjects. Judges are not free to do as they please, because they participate in (and accept) a legal tradition whose precepts they are constrained to obey. The Court majority, for example, said that "millennia of moral teaching" bar the idea that homosexual sodomy is a fundamental right, whereas the minority found a more compelling theme in American constitutional history, which endorses individual rights of choice and self-definition.

To be "bound down by the chains of the constitution," as Thomas Jefferson once put it,[4] leaves much room for creative argument. New circumstances, including new attitudes, new visions of freedom and responsibility, bring fresh meanings to abstract clauses. The hermeneutic imperative makes the Constitution a "living" instrument.

The Rule of Law

In political life, every private person and every official is supposed to be guided by legal norms of moral ordering. This practice has broad and narrow meanings. Narrowly understood, the rule of law sets limits to what may be lawfully done. As Lord Dicey put it, "The rule of law is contrasted with every system of government based on the exercise by persons in authority of wide, arbitrary, or discretionary powers of constraint."[5] Official acts must be justified by explicit or implicit grants of authority; no one can be punished in the absence of a preexisting rule that such conduct is unlawful. This posture emphasizes what *cannot* be done. However, more positive implications are easy to discern. As a moral ideal, the rule of law is a standpoint from which to judge a rule or policy, invoking standards that a purportedly lawful act must meet and affirming ideals of legitimacy, fairness, equality, and rationality. What these ideals mean and demand is always subject to interpretation and potentially informed by new understandings—for example, the meaning of "cruel and unusual" punishment. Inquiry into principles is required, one that criticizes rules and serves the common good.

Democracy and Deliberation

In a democracy the people are supposed to be sovereign; *their* will must be done. How is the will of the people to be determined? What makes *vox populi* an expression of *vox dei*? One answer invokes the authority of reason (or an idea, such as John Dewey's, of collective intelligence) to criticize and correct conventional beliefs. This includes standards of coherence and logic as well as standards required for success. For example, with respect to gardening or teaching, what is reasonable depends on what should be done to get good results: in gardening, watering, weeding, pruning, fertilizing; in teaching, preparation, clarity, patience. We move from democracy understood as *unjudged* popular rule to *deliberative* democracy, which encourages criticism and debate.

Deliberation evaluates popular decisions. The relevant ideal is not liberty but *ordered* liberty. Undefined self-government is vulnerable to groups that sometimes employ deceptive arguments or strategies. Self-government is a *normative* idea, which can be debased as well as realized.

Representative Government

Winston Churchill once said of democracy that it is "the worst form of government except all the rest." The democratic ideal is not popular or consensual. It is self-preserving and based on revocable consent. The people can act only by representation, so the quality of representation determines the quality of democracy.

A common form of representation is majority rule. The will of the majority is the will of all. To be a satisfactory expression of democracy, however, majority rule must allow free debate and accept legitimate opposition, so that present minorities may become majorities. Moreover, "the people" are not unattached individuals; they belong to subgroups with shared interests and outlooks. For majority rule to be effective *and* self-preserving, it should be responsive to group attitudes and intentions. A "mechanical" majority is a majority coherent and enduring enough to run roughshod over opponents and shut off debate. One suggested remedy for this failing of majority rule is proportional representation, which empowers minorities but fragments the political community. The moral worth of majority rule depends on how well it fosters collective intelligence.

Varieties of Representation

In the eighteenth century a thoughtful member of the British House of Commons, Edmund Burke, later recognized as an eminent political thinker, described the roles and duties of a parliamentary representative.

Burke distinguished representation as simple *agency*—doing the bidding of a principal—from agency more broadly conceived as fidelity to a process and a larger interest. He thus directed attention away from subjective *will* and toward objective *judgment*. Both are necessary for representation. Although the legislator is chosen by defined electors, it is up to him to discern the true interests of his constituents. These are duties of independence, not subservience; the difference is between obeying a will and making an independent judgment.

Burke's ideas do not preclude political compromise, constituency service, or parliamentary leadership. Since the member is a politician as well as a statesman, he will seek to be both effective in Parliament and popular in his district. The demands of political success are not ignored, but they are subordinated to a higher principle of fidelity and self-scrutiny.

Representation as Responsiveness

A special form of representation is responsive government. A potentially harmful form of responsiveness is *client-centered* administration, which serves the special wants or needs of a particular interest, at some cost to the public good. We cannot reject all client-centered policy, but we should not ignore its dangers. If a particular constituency is strong enough to *determine* public policy, the pattern may be more opportunistic than responsive, and the government's ability to reconcile special interests and the common good may be compromised. An example might be when the interests of industrial polluters are served, but the claim of environmental protection is lost. Responsiveness is a troublesome ideal because it tries to combine concern for a selected interest with fidelity to the community as a whole. But the ambiguity cannot be avoided.

Control as Regulation

The morality of governance is tested by the ways in which private activities are controlled. The powers of government are limited by a postulate of the intrinsic worth of persons, families, schools, businesses, and other components of civil society. According to that doctrine, the virtues of social life are not mainly created by government. They stem mainly from kinship, religion, trade, and manufacture. These are wellsprings of trust, cooperation, reciprocity, and energy. These virtues can be *nourished*, but they cannot be commanded.

Regulation is a kind of social control. We do not try to "regulate" crime, except when illegal activities, such as gambling or loitering, have some claim to toleration, at least in certain places or at certain times. Regulation presumes that the regulated activity has worth and deserves protection. The aim of regulation is not complete suppression. Rather, regulation limits the negative effects of otherwise desirable or tolerable activities. For example, we regulate traffic to eliminate congestion and unsafe driving. In this view it is not right to counterpose state and society. A genuine regard for civil society treats spontaneous ordering as the infrastructure of freedom and safety.

The totalitarian systems of the twentieth century tried to control every facet of society, including political association and belief. That purpose was only partly realized, since more primordial forces were always present. In the Polish Solidarity movement of the 1970s, the phrase "civil society" became a watchword and a slogan.

A blurred line between state and society is a theme that runs through much of twentieth-century thought. The need for regulation is accepted, not as rule-bound conformity but rather as a spur to willing conformity and cooperation. In responsive regulation, rules and penalties are less important than expertise and sound policy. An important theme in modern management theory holds that supervision as *help* is more effective than supervision as *command*. Responsive regulation requires knowledge of how legislative bodies or regulatory agencies work. Here again, an empiricist spirit is a necessary ingredient of humanist science.

Conflict, Consensus, and the Common Good

The morality of government largely depends on how it deals with disagreement and discord. A democratic political community expects many conflicts of interest and outlook. Unconditional loyalty and uncritical obedience are signs of domination—a pathology of governance, not a realization of its promise. The ideal is maximum feasible *self*-regulation, summoned and sustained by ideals found "in nature." A rich diversity of activities makes societies pluralist but also potentially divided.

Liberals, anarchists, and other defenders of freedom treat unity as a sham if it is not based on free association. A *claimed* consensus, furthermore, is suspect. Disagreements are mostly benign; they stem from the autonomous pursuit of legitimate interests. Good order ("eunomics" in Lon Fuller's idiom[6]) is emergent, not imposed. High levels of cooperation are more likely to be won by satisfying interests—especially elementary needs for acknowledgment and security—than by demands for conformity.

A principal finding of modern social science is that social order is better understood, and more effective and secure, when unity is emergent rather than imposed. The special virtue of an emergent order is the reconciliation of unity and diversity. Pierre-Joseph Proudhon made this point when he said that liberty is the *mother* of order, not its offspring.[7] The best cooperation is voluntary, and the premise is that such cooperation is the true bearer of moral worth. This anarchist insight is consistent with the principle that power must be checked by countervailing power, including varying ideologies or self-justifying outlooks.

A favorite liberal strategy finds consensus in *procedure*, rather than *substance*. Controversies occur within agreed-upon frameworks as to how disagreements should be perceived and managed. Consensus on procedure creates a community within which disputes are more easily resolved. A procedural ethic upholds unity while also respecting diversity. Yet substance and procedure are not wholly separate. They form a continuum with full integration at one pole and unbridgeable division at the other. Procedures affect outcomes, and outcomes are shaped by the methods they entail.[8] These judgments are normative as well as empirical, for example, as to the beneficial or harmful effects of a referendum or a rule of evidence. A sharp separation of procedure and substance distorts judgment and misreads history.

The proceduralist view seeks to insulate government from an environing world of conflict and disagreement. It finds comfort in the concept of a "neutral" state, unencumbered by a special history or its own understanding of the public good. The idea of a neutral state is attractive in that it limits the reach of government and honors the diversity of interests. It falls short, however, as a theory of how government fosters or forsakes the common good.

Constitutions speak to both substance and procedure. A government of defined and limited powers may be vague about substantive purposes and rights, leaving much for future generations to decide. The U.S. Constitution, written in 1787, said its aims were "to form a more perfect Union . . . promote the general Welfare, and secure the Blessing of Liberty to ourselves and our Posterity." This language left plenty of room for disagreement, and new settlements, such as the New Deal legislation on labor unions and social security. American constitutional history offers many tributes to procedure, but it is also a record of struggle for wisdom about substantive issues such as slavery and women's rights. The constitutional story is at least as much about social policy as about ways of deciding contentious issues.

The common good is necessarily a proper subject for controversy, and that is why democracy calls for legitimate opposition, free speech, and open government. The larger objective is a shared understanding of social conditions and acceptable alternatives. The point is to know not who wins but what will improve the common life.

The morality of governance posits the intrinsic worth of private groups. Power is judged by that premise, and strong government is accepted, but government that rejects legitimate interests is not.

7

Rationality and Responsibility

IN THIS CHAPTER I explore a common failing in social life and thought: the conflict between rationality and moral responsibility. Fidelity to purpose has many benefits, but it fosters a retreat from responsibility. This tension affects business, law, politics, education, and military planning—wherever a specialized technique trumps or replaces moral judgment.

In the nineteenth century, a "romantic" reaction against the eighteenth century found moral worth in history, culture, localism, and nationalism. All were valued as sources of harmony, wholeness, and rootedness. This perspective undermined rationality in that it is divorced from fellowship and commitment.

Even in economics, the natural home of single-minded rationality, concepts like "opportunity cost" and "externalities" pointed to benefits forgone and burdens overlooked in the pursuit of natural economic ends. The concept of "unintended consequences" places rational conduct within a natural order, subject to distortion and missed opportunity.[1]

The Natural History of Rationality

As a way of acting and knowing, rationality is something more than an abstract idea. Rationality should be understood as a contingent and variable mode of action or decision, which responds in knowable ways to congenial or uncongenial conditions. The standards of rationality, such as fidelity to purpose and calculation of costs, arise from the demands and limits of specialized activity. As Herbert Simon has said, rationality is "bounded by circumstances that fix goals and limit alternatives."[2] Especially important is the preference for clear and proximate goals and for technical rather than political judgments. These dispositions focus attention and discipline choice, as in building a bridge, marketing a product, or conducting a military operation.

The natural history of rationality stems from precise goals and expertise. Whatever interferes—perhaps by invoking *multiple* goals and *ancillary* interests—is "noise," to be ignored or referred to "leaders" whose task it is to find a "higher" rationality by taking account of unintended and long-term effects. Leaders accept responsibility for outcomes that lie beyond the pursuit of sharply defined goals.

This dynamic has not gone unnoticed, as in Simon's concept of "bounded" rationality. We should also attend to Max Weber's analysis of *Verantwortungsethik*—the "ethic of responsibility"—which he contrasted to an "ethic of conviction," or *Gesinnungsethik*. An ethic of responsibility looks to the welfare of a particular group or community, and is no great friend of consistency, which is no virtue when changing circumstances redefine collective needs or when multiple and often conflicting interests are accommodated. In an ethic of conviction, rationality is found in logic and principle. "Who says A," one hears, "must say B." An ethic of responsibility is less troubled by inconsistency and cares more about outcomes for persons, institutions, and communities. Weber identified different kinds of rationality, prized for different reasons and subject to characteristic failings, capable of seizing some opportunities while missing others.

Myopic Rationality

The chief features of rational conduct—purposes clearly defined, alternatives well understood, costs calculated—favor an *atomistic* conception of responsibility. Therefore, willful insularity prevails. Rationality is indeed hard to come by when boundaries are unclear or when commitments are open-ended. As "purpose" becomes "mission," decision makers are liberated by being granted freedom from "irrelevant" constraints. A carefully drawn contract fixes obligations and allows costs to be calculated, including the cost of a breach. In a going concern, however, obligations are not so neatly defined or understood. They arise not from the terms of an agreement but from the realities of interdependence. In business, for example, the claims of "regular" employees, suppliers, and customers are accommodated, perhaps by providing security of employment or special discounts.

These and other findings of social science reveal conditions that encourage or limit responsibility. Such inquiries reflect the ethos of humanist science in that they encourage a close connection to moral philosophy, supported by empirical inquiry into kinds and contingencies.

In a law-governed community we find a strain toward "formal" justice, which is an example of myopic rationality. Judges and lawyers rely on received categories, made plain by legal training. Specialized learning fosters precision, but the outcome is marred by a trained incapacity to know and remedy the pathologies generated by formalist thinking. In response, "legal realism" advocates more empirical and policy-sensitive doctrines, rejecting the idea that rationality is more attuned to purity of doctrine than to the identification of interests and the release of energies.

Modern economics tries to improve the rationality of business and government by favoring policies that enhance free exchange in unfettered markets. At the same time, economics claims *descriptive* validity, based on a key assumption about the prevalence and salience of self-interest. This premise is easy to accept because much public policy takes for granted that people generally act in favor of what seems to serve their near-term needs and wants. Thus if savings are encouraged, perhaps by lowered taxes, investment will increase; if interest rates are low, demand for durable goods will rise; if prices are high, people will look for cheaper alternatives. These generalizations, though largely valid, are far from the whole truth, which depends on how we understand self-interest. Narrowly conceived, as the pursuit of maximum benefits at least cost, self-interest does not account for status-driven consumption or long-term strategies. When emotions are in play, or when economic or political choices are unclear, the meaning of self-interest is obscured. Alexis de Tocqueville wrote of "self-interest rightly understood"—that is, informed by norms of self-respect and propriety.

Economic myopia is overcome insofar as preferences are *evaluated* rather than merely accepted as given. A critique of preferences is likely to invoke principles of responsible choice. Preferences are examined for irrationalities and distortions; business activity is assessed for its integrity and effects on other spheres, as when the public interest in a nurturing environment is neglected.

Rational myopia is a natural by-product of specialized activity. It stems not from folly or narrow self-interest but from the realities of association and participation. The chief benefit is narrowed responsibility, often justified by a "purely" military, political, economic, educational, or scientific "logic."

This "retreat to technology"[3] accounts for recurrent appeals for more holistic and contextual ways of thinking. In medicine, for example, a holistic approach attends to the patient's total condition—physical, mental, social—instead of relying on narrowly focused technical tools, such as surgery or pharmacology. In this view, if death is imminent, it is allowed to happen. In effect, a philosophy of life is brought to bear as a moral framework for medical practice. Holism is a voice of resistance to technocratic and myopic rationality.

Rationality and Reason

Although "reason" and "rationality" are related ideas, they are not synonyms. Their conflation was tolerable in the eighteenth century because the great task of the "age of reason" was to open minds closed by unreflective custom and belief. The difference between rationality and reason could be safely ignored. In time, however, the claims of reason have become distinct. Rationality is *subordinated* to reason, whose authority is extended to the choice of *ends* as well as *means*. Ends chosen in the light of reason are judged in part by the means they entail; reason, however, reveals the interdependence and interplay of means and ends. A corollary is that practices and policies should be *efficient* as well as *effective*. Efficiency takes into account hidden costs and unintended effects. In military operations, for example, it may be effective to destroy an urban target, but extensive "collateral damage" is unacceptable; in business, efficiency is affected by the imperatives of maintaining employee morale and customer satisfaction. Reason holds rationality to standards that embrace multifaceted concerns and lasting effects.

The subordination of rationality to reason is a recurrent theme among modern writers. A distinction is sometimes drawn between "instrumental" and "substantive" reason. Instrumental reason chooses means to unexamined ends, while substantive reason governs the choice of goals as well as methods, a strategy that includes conceptions of "nature"—e.g., the nature of deliberation, policing, or public opinion.

A cognate distinction between "objective" and "subjective" reason, or between "abstract" and "concrete" reason, has been suggested. These are simply other ways of saying that rationality is subject to criticism in the light of reason. In jurisprudence we have learned, with the help of Ronald Dworkin, that in a modern legal system *principles* are authoritative resources for interpreting *rules*.[4]

Horizons of Self-Interest

The best-known form of rationality is self-interested conduct, such as an increased profit margin or market share or freedom to marry in accordance with one's preferences. We can take for granted that most people most of the time will do what self-interest suggests. Yet this pursuit of happiness is often shortsighted and self-destructive. Genuine self-interest may be elusive, or obscured by a paucity of good choices.

In an expanded view of self-interest, the satisfactions that people seek include self-esteem and the regard of their fellows, goals that act as reliable spurs to effort and cooperation. In this way, self-interest reaches beyond individual benefits to more comprehensive and collective advantages.

Widening horizons is a prominent theme in social psychology, and the values at stake are readily discerned. George Herbert Mead described a transition from a morality of the "significant other" to one of what he called the "generalized other," which emerges when people come to understand and accept general principles rather than specific rules or edicts. In contrast, a morality of the "significant other" is defined and enforced by people who matter in our lives: parents, friends, teachers, or employers. The "generalized other" conveys what it means to be fair, cooperative, kind, or reverent. These ways of knowing what moral conduct requires are learned in play, at school, and at work. Children respond mainly to authority figures who share the experiences of belonging and participation. The morality of the "significant other" is parochial and self-limiting, cabined by connection and wary of strangers.

Varieties of Responsibility

The enlargement of self-interest is a gateway to social and moral responsibility, bridging the gap between self-regard and regard for others, blurring the line between identity and well-being. This expanded meaning is wholly compatible with valuing *individuality*, but not with *individualism*. Although self-interest is transformed by interdependence and shared consciousness, people remain separate and unique. The changes take place within particular contexts, each of which has its own norms of care and loyalty, its own ethic of responsibility.

In economic thought, the question is asked, Can rationality restrain uninhibited self-seeking? Is there a blind spot in Adam Smith's image of the self-regarding merchant who benefits mankind not by acts of altruism but by furthering his own interest? In Smith's scenario, altruism and self-interest reinforce one another. However, virtuous conduct is mostly not single-minded. Rather, it is sensitive to the claims of multiple interests. All conduct has ancillary, unintended, often unwanted effects. What we do for one purpose affects neighboring interests, positively or negatively. Maximizing a single goal or benefit produces a degree of tunnel vision, limiting attention to other interests. In theory, maximization may take account of any condition or constraint. In fact, however, it is not an innocent or merely heuristic idea. Maximization leads to diminished responsibility for at least some unplanned outcomes.

A realistic and value-centered rule takes account of *all* costs, including costs created by multiple and changing purposes. The costs of public higher education, for example, include career counseling and athletic programs, whose "necessity" stems from custom, pride, and the expectations of students, parents, and alumni. In a large corporation, the "cost of doing business" includes employee training and the correction of "negative externalities" such as pollution or dangerous facilities. Some of these costs are imposed by public agencies, others by business necessities, such as public relations and investor confidence.[5]

These realities affect initiative, innovation, and the quality of production.

THE ABOVE DISCUSSION is a humanist critique of technocratic mentality. The argument is not new. In the twentieth century, a number of theorists—Alfred Weber, Martin Heidegger, Jacques Ellul, Siegfried Giedion, and Michel Foucault—have called attention to the insidious effects on morality and culture of a preoccupation with "technique." When technology dominates perception and policy, that which has intrinsic worth is lost from view. Technology detaches means and ends. The virtues of rationality are not ignored, but the idea is to limit excess by resisting the reduction of value to preference and of well-being to utility. The true measure of success is the quality of human life. Economics, politics, education, urban planning—these and many other activities are exposed to the menace of uncontrolled technique. Technical sophistication is paid for by restricted vision and responsibility. This outcome is fostered by a failure to recognize or take seriously the true costs of purpose-driven action.

A remedy is suggested in the "dialectical imagination" described by Hegel, Marx, and their posterity.[6] According to that intellectual tradition, dialectical thinking leaves the abstract realms of discourse and enters a more concrete social and historical experience. This way of thinking enlarges latent tensions or "contradictions," as in Freud's theory of personality and

Marx's theory of capitalism. In these writings, the urgencies of personality and the forces of history replace the logic of disputation.

A dialectical imagination pervades the writings of John Dewey, who argued against "pernicious dualisms" such as fact and value, body and mind, theory and practice, thought and observation, ends and means.[7] The dichotomies are pernicious insofar as they block inquiry into the interaction and interdependence of facts and ideas. A capacious conception of "nature" includes all that knowledge can tell us, in the form of "warranted assertions," about the experienced world. Nature displays subtle patterns of adaptation and problem solving, some of which sow discord, while others are more harmonious.

A dialectical imagination highlights the paradoxical and tension-laden complexity of human existence, where evil is done in the name of good, where special loyalties are transcended as moral horizons expand. This humanist sensibility points to the complexity and fluidity of human life and accords with many insights of philosophy and theology. It retains, however, a steady focus on the *wholeness*, *integrity*, and *individuality* of persons and groups. A humanist perspective is not necessarily optimistic. Rather, it is comfortable with the idea of "original sin," understood as arising from primordial impulses and desires.

Dewey's rejection of "pernicious dualisms" is part of his "instrumentalism," which is an alternative name for his philosophy. However, instrumentalism does not exalt "technique." For Dewey, ideas are tools for sorting and connecting aspects of a natural world; they have intellectual worth insofar as they are useful for enriching lives and gaining mastery over a recalcitrant and indifferent world. "Technique" avoids responsibility for the full range of outcomes. The lesson is that ideas can be blinders as well as binoculars.

Rejecting a radical separation of means and ends, pragmatic humanism subjects technology to criteria of social and personal well-being. Every technical scheme should be modified to accommodate contending interests. In this way, *reason* trumps *rationality*, extending the reach of responsibility.

Dewey's analysis also counters the reduction of *value* to *utility*, as in the equation of love and sex. What responsibility requires and to whom it is directed depend on the context, and can be known only by empirical study of the settings within which values are realized or endangered. In an interdependent world, fidelity to purpose—disciplined pursuit of predefined goals—is subject to norms of responsibility.

8

The Quality of Culture

THE SOCIAL SCIENCE OF CULTURE, notably cultural anthropology, is value-centered and shares major preoccupations with the humanities. A chief objective is to identify and analyze distinctive ways of life, manifested in diverse understandings of kinship, religion, authority, and selfhood. These findings have an explicit moral lesson: every culture deserves respect as an expression of human need and creativity. In rejecting ethnocentrism, anthropology has fostered humility and rebuked parochial pride. This teaching affirms a universalist ethic based on appreciation for a common humanity.

Humanism and Anthropology

A salient difference between humanist and anthropological conceptions of culture is the *selective* stance of the humanist view. In that perspective only a part of a society's activities are cultural. Moreover, culture can be *evaluated* as well as described. In contrast, the anthropological view is neither selective nor evaluative. Culture is the entire social heritage or, as Alfred Kroeber put it, "that which the human species has and other social species lack: speech, knowledge, belief, custom, art, technology, ideals, and rules . . . what we learn from other men, from our elders and the past, plus what we may add to it."[1]

The omnibus character of the anthropological concept stems from a special intellectual history. For many years a chief concern of social science was to set off the cultural from the biological, thus acknowledging the great impact of social experience on how people live, what they think. In countering biological determinism anthropologists were undertaking a task of no particular interest to humanists. It was obvious to them that people owe everything to their histories. The main challenge was to understand the *quality* of culture and account for variations in forms and achievements.

Humanism is explicitly evaluative. It makes sense to say that some groups are more cultured than others, that some universal values are explained by objective conditions, and that ethnocentrism is variable and not inescapable. Communities differ in the extent to which they are ethnocentric or, instead, encourage humane and universal values.

Wary of ethnocentrism, anthropologists eschew evaluation. To be human, they say, is to have a culture, and we are all culture-bound. Therefore, judgments of the worth or quality of culture are necessarily ethnocentric. If we judge another culture negatively, it is because our own culture has affected our thoughts and preferences. If we judge it positively, that is due to a convergence of outlooks and values. We are all culture-bound, all limited by ethnocentric and ethnomorphic ideas.

Cultures "Thin" and "Thick"

A discordant note was struck by Edward Sapir (1884–1939), a Yale anthropologist and a founder of descriptive linguistics, when he wrote:

A genuine culture is not necessarily high or low; it is merely inherently harmonious, balanced, and self-satisfactory: a richly varied and yet somehow unified and consistent attitude toward life. A genuine culture is, ideally speaking, a culture in which nothing is spiritually meaningless, in which no important part of the general functioning brings with it a sense of frustration, of misdirected or unsympathetic effort.[2]

Here a nonjudgmental attitude—rejecting the idea that one set of practices or attitudes is "higher" or "lower" than others—is made compatible with assessing a culture's wholeness, harmony, and the satisfactions or frustrations it brings. Sapir refers to *quality*, not *content*. The analysis of quality requires judgment and brings humanist values to bear. At bottom is a theory of human nature: how people respond to disharmony and stress and how their lives are impoverished or enriched in work, play, kinship, and community. Like many students of preliterate communities, Sapir was sensitive to the distress and decay often brought about by Western influence and domination. He concluded that cultures can be dysfunctional or, in his idiom, "spurious."

Alienation

A concern for the quality of culture is a recurrent theme in the thought of many students of Western modernity. An example is Karl Marx's theory of alienation.[3] Marx argued that the kinds of work required in capitalist industry result in feelings of resentment and disengagement. He called this condition *Entfremdung* or "alienation," which is a state of mind and spirit that accounts for problems of discipline, absenteeism, and other indicators of low morale. Alienation is a sign of crushed individuality and the lack of satisfying, life-enhancing work. Only new forms of employment, rejecting domination, will be compatible with self-realization and self-respect. The remedy for alienation is humane work and cooperation.[4]

Modernization

Many have found in modern history what Max Weber called the "disenchantment" (*Entzauberung*) of the world. Several master trends have weakened bonds of kinship, place, occupation, and religion: separation of work and household, secularization of belief and practice, growing preoccupation with rational coordination in major institutions. These trends, it was thought, threaten selfhood, debase expressive symbolism, and create a thinned, or attenuated, culture in which the pull of kinship and locality is diminished and institutions are more remote and opaque. This fraying of social bonds evokes last-ditch efforts to preserve a lost coherence. The nuclear family, though never wholly absent, becomes more isolated and detached; holy days are holidays; a consumerist desire for three-day weekends trumps celebration of heroes' or founders' birthdays, which are "observed" on nearby Mondays.

In the attenuated culture of modernity, the world becomes more impersonal, more readily manipulated, less easily invested with intrinsic worth. When the texture of social life thins, human resources are lost; isolation is more prevalent. This diagnosis is not necessarily a rejection of modernity, but it says that many important values are harder to sustain. The benefits of modernity are won at some cost to solidarity and satisfaction.

A "thick" culture, on the other hand, is a densely woven fabric of meanings and attachments. Strong ties to distant relatives are felt and shed a benign light on nepotistic practices. In a thick culture, identities are strong and multiple sources of self-respect exist. Fulfillment of obligations is a welcome conformity rather than a burden. Despite suffering and sacrifice, obedience is an honor and a source of pride and satisfaction. In a thick culture of, say, military life, fellow soldiers and sailors are buddies and shipmates, for whom feelings of affection are appropriate.

A thick culture transforms systems of rational and impersonal coordination into habitats replete with person-centered meanings. When solidarity depends only on rules and commands, obedience and zeal are problematic. A culture based on more personal connections—to symbols, leaders, colleagues, practices—is more likely to enhance cohesion and effectiveness. This is the great prize sought by leaders of purpose-driven groups. They seek a thick culture, enriched by many varied subcultures, each contributing in its own way to shared goals.

A thick culture is not self-justifying, nor is it, as Sapir said, necessarily "high" or "low." Such a culture may serve unwanted ends or do so by illicit means. These patterns do not diminish the significance, for all participants, of a culture thickened by meaningful symbols and satisfying practices. Whether a culture is thick or thin does not necessarily determine its moral worth. For example, a criminal "family" or a terrorist group may well have a thick and coherent culture.

Signs of Convergence

Although the social science and humanist conceptions of culture have been different and even counterposed, some intellectual impulses bring them together. In 1958 Alfred Kroeber and Talcott Parsons noted that the important nineteenth-century task was to distinguish social from biological heredity, and in that effort sociologists and anthropologists cooperated. Sociologists used the omnibus idea of "society," while anthropologists used the equally omnibus term "culture." "We suggest," they wrote, "that it is useful to define the concept *culture* for most usages more narrowly than has been generally the case in the American anthropological tradition, restricting its reference to transmitted and created content and patterns of *values, ideas, and other symbolic-meaningful systems*. On the other hand we suggest that the term *society*—or more generally *social system*—be used to designate the specifically *relational* system of interactions among individuals and collectivities."[5]

Here a selective rather than an omnibus concept of culture receives support among theorists, and what is selected gives prominence to the ideal, the symbolic, and the meaningful.

Social Learning

In what we may call the Standard Version, culture is the whole of a community's (or group's or epoch's) attitudes, ideas, and practices. We cannot wholly reject this perspective because there is much to be learned from the description and analysis of accepted ways of doing things—of working, cooking, hospitality. These "folkways" and "mores," learned in the course of growing up, show how much is attributable to social learning rather than to biological inheritance. The salience of social learning was a major theme in late-nineteenth-century social science, and for much of the twentieth century as well. An omnibus conception of culture was appealing, largely because students of society were keen to stress that culture is a product of history, not race. Nevertheless, despite rampant diversity in history and culture, human animals have "psychic unity." This common humanity coexists comfortably with manifest differences in custom and outlook.

Expressive Symbolism

The conclusions just noted are especially important for the study of expressive symbolism, which is mainly *connotative* rather than *denotative*. A flag may be just a banner, denoting a particular country, group, or institution. It may also carry associations that enlarge and enrich that denotative meaning. Feelings of loyalty and respect are evoked, including rules for proper ways of displaying the flag or discarding it. To burn the flag as an act of protest will be met by charges of sacrilege. In short, a flag can be a sacred object, not merely a useful or profane one.

Much the same may be said of symbolism in religion and related contexts, such as the oath-taking ceremonies of marriage, office-holding, or testimony. A cross may be, for nonbelievers, a particular arrangement of lines or grids, but for the Christian communicant, the cross evokes holy events and teachings.

The Culture-Creating Act

The psychological root of expressive symbolism is a human impulse to *escape impersonality*, achieved by investing the world with person-centered meanings. The primordial culture-creating act transforms an impersonal setting—natural or man-made—into one that has significance for human fears and hopes. Encounters with impersonality are ever-present sources of anxiety and even dread, whereas an impersonal environment frustrates the wish to be acknowledged as having intrinsic worth.

Expressive symbols heighten emotions and fortify attachments. Ceremony and myth make the world comprehensible and friendly, and feelings of humility, awe, reverence, pride, and obedience are encouraged, even for commitment to personal and communal events. Ceremonies seal important occasions and heighten emotional responses. In a thinned or attenuated culture, expressive symbolism is diminished or forgone.

A Strain Toward the Aesthetic

A strong connection between "culture" and "high culture" is fostered by expressive symbolism. Painting, sculpture, dance, poetry, song, architecture—all are potent ways of deepening meanings and intensifying emotions. Patriotism and divine worship are bolstered by works of art that enhance the epiphanies of everyday life. Such choreographed rituals add intensity to expressive symbolism. Special buildings, arches, and monuments evoking awe and pride in "impartial and implacable" justice become cultural artifacts. Courts and legislative halls are made splendid palaces.

Expressive symbols are variably effective, some more capable than others of eliciting appropriate feelings of attachment or reverence. Artists are specialists in creating such symbols, in that effectiveness depends on combining economy and richness—economy of statement and richness of connotative meaning. Economy is needed for evocative clarity, as in a shimmering tower or an idealized sculpture. To be an effective *cultural* symbol, however, the abstraction must convey a compelling message of majesty or divinity.

The Quality of Experience

The argument just made draws inspiration from the ideas of John Dewey, who distinguished experience-in-general from "having an experience."[6] In *an* experience, something stands out as a unified event or concept of experience—in general, more conventional, unengaging, readily forgotten experiences. Here Dewey strikes an existentialist note: having an experience is not the same as merely being alive. Rather, it heightens response and focuses attention. The distinction is normative but not arbitrary or culture-bound, nor is it a uniquely human value. Dewey pointed out that the hungry animal stalking its prey is in a state of being that is different from that of an animal reacting to random stimuli. The urgencies of hunger or fear focus attention and awareness. A hitherto neutral environment becomes alive with threat and promise.

Dewey's fundamental interest was epistemological. There is, he thought, an ultimate interdependence of cognition and valuation. This points us in the right direction, but Dewey characteristically did not pay enough attention to the ways in which humans *differ* from other animals. Many species have experiences and apprehend meanings, but the human animal has a distinctive tendency to *seek out* meaningful experiences and find ways of extending and supporting them.

Dewey's argument does not *distinguish* culture and high culture. Although high culture elaborates and perfects expressive symbolism, it has no monopoly on its creation. A cultural symbol is not necessarily an aesthetic achievement. A village square or churchyard, a leader's birthplace, a treasured stand of trees—all may be cultural symbols without being works of art. To say there is a *strain* or *disposition* does not mean that every expressive symbol has aesthetic worth. Nor is art the only, or even the main, vehicle of symbolic expression. Many well-established customs, such as heterosexual marriage, or a preferred style of architecture may have cultural significance without having much aesthetic value. Independence Hall in Philadelphia is not notable as a work of art, but it is preserved as an expressive symbol of a treasured history. Similarly, the Vietnam Memorial in Washington, D.C., gains symbolic power from a visitor's opportunity to find and touch the names of friends or relatives killed in the war; in the nearby Lincoln Memorial, the brooding figure of President Lincoln adds its eloquence to the mighty words graven on the walls. Public displays of memory and appreciation connect culture and high culture. A historian who seeks successfully to depict the spirit or ethos of an epoch or community is likely to enter the realm of expressive symbolism.

Culture and Civilization

The idea that cultures are unique and self-justifying has been a high barrier for those who wish to characterize some practices and outlooks as more "civilized" than others. The German historian Alfred Weber (1868–1958) dealt with this problem by identifying "civilization" with technological advance. The idea of "progress" is indeed less troublesome if it refers to technological invention, thereby detaching it from custom and belief. A technique of construction, transportation, communication, or warfare can be judged higher or lower, more or less advanced, if one technique is more effective or efficient than another, without necessarily judging its moral or cultural significance.

This strategy preserves the commonsense understanding of "progress" without giving up the core of relativism. Relevant ideas are appealing, but our ordinary language points to a deeper truth. Civilization should be understood as an offspring of "civility," which connotes respect, self-restraint, and reflection. People are civilized, not by virtue of the tools they use, or the speed and convenience of travel, but insofar as they adhere to norms of forbearance and regard for others. We recognize civilization in attitudes of toleration and inclusion, in practices of cooperation, dialogue, hospitality, and courtesy. There are many ways of being hospitable, and some, like wife lending, are hard for *us* to accept, though we do understand that different forms of greeting or sharing meals are likely to arise in different circumstances. We can appreciate the impulse and respect the practice without incorporating such practices in our lives.

The moral ideal of civilization transcends contexts of work, war, politics, and parenting. Civilization is manifest in the so-called laws of war, that is, in standards governing the treatment of prisoners and non-combatants. Thus, even warfare can be civilized if victors and vanquished accept restraints and treat each other respectfully.

The Limits of Relativism

Cultural relativism is the main moral teaching of modern cultural anthropology. According to that view, all our judgments are products of "enculturation"—that is, they are molded by a particular culture, which has its own customs and values. Everyone is a product of cultural conditioning; everyone's judgments are limited and tainted by cultural sources of mind and self. We transcend those limits by education and diversity.

This teaching has a vital assumption: that people are *alike* in important ways. This view calls for compassion for their troubles, respect for their ways, and admiration for their achievements. The moral teaching of relativism combines valuing diversity with appreciating special needs and aspirations.

Radical and Responsible Relativism

We should distinguish radical relativism from a more qualified, moderate, and responsible version of relativism. Radical relativism asserts that all judgments are subjective products of enculturation or conditioning. It does not heed persistent reminders of cultural universals. Long lists of commonalities have been drawn up, including division of labor, leadership, friendship, kinship, hospitality, mental health, and much else. All cultures have systems of family and kinship; all protect and discipline children; all distinguish fact from fantasy; all know how to perform elementary tasks of farming and animal husbandry; all have rules for determining ownership of land and chattel. "All cultures define as abnormal people who consistently fail to maintain some degree of control over their impulse life."[7]

Moderate relativism holds that judgments are indeed contextual but are also based on principles that transcend those contexts, thus presuming a normative framework of justification or excuse. An example is the idea (discussed above) that a culture may be thin or thick, attenuated or well integrated. Such judgments do not speak mainly to *content*—for example, beliefs about divinity; they refer instead to the quality of human relations and of symbolic experience. Cultures may be compared and assessed as more or less capable of educating children to become competent adults. Moreover, certain practices may be justified and accounted for by, for example, scarcity of food and exploitation. The qualifications show that bad practices are controlled by standards that reflect shared concerns about infants, women, and mental disability, standards that transcend and are modified by the demands of contexts.

Cultural relativism rests upon—but is also limited by—a theory of common humanity. All people are alike in vital respects: born of copulation, vulnerable to disease and death, and desirous of love, respect, and at least some form of admiration.

The human animal thrives or withers under congenial or uncongenial conditions. Especially important is the attribution of intrinsic worth and distinctive identity. This particularity is a universal feature of human life. Social life is mainly local, a condition that has costs as well as benefits. Therefore we should not *counterpose* the particular and the universal. Instead we should learn how each contributes to the benefits and limits of collective life. When William Graham Sumner said, "the mores can make anything right,"[8] he was offering an arresting slogan but a dubious truth. In fact, as Sumner well understood, custom is a historical outcome of recurrent experience and adaptation. The conclusions show concern for physical health and moral well-being. Because the parameters of well-being are objective, the mores cannot make *anything* right. Custom takes account of human frailties and capacities.

Radical relativism claims the cachet of comparative research, but it closes doors to what can be learned from cross-cultural study of personality. Although contexts do matter, they are subject to principles based on more comprehensive understandings of behavior.

Social scientists who teach "the psychic unity of mankind" cannot accept radical relativism. No convincing case can be made for major differences in practical affairs, including what it means to be prudent, cooperative, or rational. Without knowing these commonalities, we cannot know what problems are set by diverse practices and beliefs.

9

Law and Justice

THE CENTRALITY OF IDEALS AND STANDARDS is well exemplified in jurisprudence, the social science of law and justice. This work has mainly consisted of analytical, historical, and comparative research. Jurisprudence is not the same as learning to "think like a lawyer"—that is, to grasp the rules implicit in judicial decisions and the varieties of legal authority. Jurisprudence studies the sources of law and the variable authority of legal precepts.

In recent years, a "law and society" movement has brought these matters more firmly into social science. Legal orders are seen as integral, many-faceted parts of the social landscape, calling for systematic study of the conditions that affect legal forms, procedures, and ideals. A premise is that law *in action* is distinguished from law *on the books*. Law "in action" refers to official behavior as it responds to the ambient contexts, which affect those who make, interpret, and enforce the law. Each context has its own constraints and temptations, influencing the course and integrity of official decisions. Social science turns a critical eye on the interplay of legal ideals and social realities.

A humanist science of justice combines description and evaluation. Descriptive facts tell us when and how ideals are realized or imperiled;

normative inquiry clarifies ideals and explores their connections to each other and to more fundamental principles.

The Claims of Justice

A close connection between law and justice is proclaimed by much expressive symbolism. A main purpose of the United States Constitution is "to establish Justice"; the attorney general heads the Department of Justice; a judge of the Supreme Court is a "justice"; on the Court's palace is a frieze reading, "Equal justice under law."

That laws are not necessarily just is recognized in ordinary as well as scholarly language. Scholars speak of "positive" law as referring to enactments or decisions of duly established bodies such as a legislature, court, or regulatory agency. These decisions are distinguished by more general and elusive principles, such as impartiality and consistency with a moral and legal heritage. If a statute or decision does not meet those standards, it may be interpreted narrowly or even annulled. The idea of "positive" law implies that law may be defective and its claim to authority denied. In a developed legal system, positive law is scrutinized by reviewing bodies, such as appellate courts; or may languish, uncited and unenforced, as "dead letter." The opportunity to criticize, revise, or reject positive law takes us from law to justice, that is, to a "higher" law of authoritative principles.

Positive law is composed mainly of rules, such as what constitutes a binding contract, a punishable offense, or a valid driver's license. Also included are the "concepts" and "doctrines" of judge-made law. The demand for a rationally defensible rule is itself a principle of justice. This "model of rules," as Ronald Dworkin called it,[1] advances justice by exposing and limiting arbitrary decisions. Governance by rules is a vital part of doing justice, but law includes more general ideas as well, which can be appealed to when rules are challenged as invalid or unjust. Positive law includes standards for criticizing a rule or decision, and judges and other officials appeal to those norms when the legal validity of a rule is questioned.

Law is not necessarily just, but it offers a *promise* of justice. Legal decisions should be impartial and mindful of reasonable expectations of people. Justice counterposes *reason* to *will*, including the will of a democratic legislature. The closer the connection between law and justice, the more opportunities there are for challenging and curbing official conduct.

In a rudimentary legal system, criticism of positive law is confined to questioning an official's authority to decide. This may sometimes require "legitimacy in depth," which scrutinizes the *use* of authority as well as its *source*. A businessman may say, "I run this business because I own it." The law may indeed recognize authority based on ownership, yet it will also examine how employees or customers are treated.

Rules are indispensable for orderly process, but they are not self-justifying. They may be promulgated by those who lack the required authority to do so, or they may be defective because they are offensive to standards of fairness or impartiality. For example, a rule requiring bikers to wear helmets may well survive scrutiny, but one requiring gloves or short pants might be considered to be an undue infringement of personal liberty. Rules may be challenged as irrational, discriminatory, or excessively burdensome. A government's rules may have a prima facie claim to obedience, but that does not save them from challenge and potential rejection.

The Rule of Law

The connection between law and justice is also part of discussions of "the rule of law," which demands fidelity to authoritative standards. Officials and ordinary citizens are not to do as they please; for example, pedestrians act lawfully by crossing streets when lights are green or by using designated crossings. Albert Dicey said the rule of law is "contrasted with every system of government based on the exercise by persons in authority of wide, arbitrary, or discretionary powers of constraint."[2] The rule of law is said to be a government of law, not men. People act honorably, and with respect for the community, when they conform their conduct to authoritative rules. Because everyone has this duty, it is said that no official, however mighty, is above the law.

The rule of law is an *affirmative* ideal, best understood as *law plus standards*. The standards are what Lon Fuller called "the morality of law": not the *utility* of a zoning, taxation, or corporate governance law but its *quality* as effective and fair. Laws that do not meet these standards are defective and may be ignored, nullified, or narrowly construed. The rule of law trumps the "black letter" rules stated pithily in legal texts and treatises. The ideal of a "rule of law" invites analysis of underlying values and utilities.

In the preceding discussion we may discern two different and in some ways contrasting ideas: negative and affirmative conceptions of the rule of law. The negative conception curbs discretion and prevents the abuse of power, a strategy that opposes reason to will, notably by conforming decisions to rules and rules to principles. Every product of *ungoverned* will is offensive to the rule of law. Any act of will, including majority will, can be scrutinized for its conformity to standards of responsibility and deliberation. These standards encourage criticism and enrich participation. However, they also lead to increased uncertainty.

An affirmative conception of the rule of law reaches beyond the well-recognized aims of restraining abuse of power, protecting the weak against the strong, providing for the peaceful settlement of disputes, and facilitating desirable transactions. The rule of law also provides frameworks within which private life can go forward. This conception upholds the dignity and integrity of individuals and groups. An ideal of "responsive" law emerges: not a rejection of rules, but a rejection of rule-*centeredness*. Even this does not fully realize the larger promise of the rule of law, however, as it explores contested meanings in legal, economic, and political theories.

Civil Society and Common Law

That law helps create an orderly social life is a major theme in the study of legal systems, including the common-law system developed in England during the late Middle Ages and found throughout the English-speaking world. "Common law" is judge-made law, supplemented by landmark statutes and constitutions. In England, the judges of the King's Bench created a law that was common partly in that it transcended local rules affecting the sale or inheritance of property, and the rights and duties of neighbors, parents, wives, children, and laborers. The king's judges were supposed to *find*—not *make*—the applicable law, and they did so by discerning the obligations and expectations of ordinary life. As "oracles" rather than legislators, judges would reveal and refine the wisdom and legacy of the community. It was the duty of common-law judges to interpret the history of the community by showing their good sense, always with an eye to the peace and prosperity of the realm. Ultimately the reasoning of judges in the course of deciding particular cases would become a distinctive feature of common-law jurisprudence. Judge-made law, though creative, was and is subject to special constraints, such as respect for precedent and a preference for incremental rather than sweeping change.

Common law is often associated with custom and tradition. However, this interpretation should yield to a more complex inquiry into *good order*. For example, a sound common-law rule clarifies parental authority as well as rules of inheritance and employment. These "customs" are defended—and often amended—in the course of deciding among claims and counterclaims. Judges were presumed to know how institutions work and what obligations they create. To be "learned in the law" was to be a perceptive and realistic analyst of social facts. This expertise, fortified by acquaintance with legal concepts and doctrines, sustained the legitimacy of the courts.

"Artificial reason," as Sir Edward Coke called it, is the common-law judge's cloak of legitimacy: the concepts, doctrines, and rules taught to lawyers as "authoritative starting-points for legal reasoning."[3] The operative word is "authoritative." Judges draw on ideas handed down by their predecessors, such as "contract," "negligence," or "trust," among many others. Artificial reason looks to logic *and* experience: to logic for clear meanings and categories, to experience for knowledge of how rights and obligations arise.

The judges have a lively concern for social well-being. They are presumed to know the basic realities of agriculture and commerce and to believe such activities are important to society and deserve protection.

In this way, law is governed by standards of well-being. All interests have value, though none has *absolute* value; all are subject to scrutiny and revision; all subordinate will to reason—that is, to society-minded interpretation of rights and duties.

What the common law is and does cannot be separated from how we understand society. According to Justice Oliver Wendell Holmes, Jr. (1841–1933), there is in social life an irrepressible struggle among contending interests. This "war of each against all" is tamed (but not extinguished) by a supreme authority. It is the duty of common-law judges to uphold that authority, which may be, in democratic systems, the will of a legislature.

In the seventeenth century, Thomas Hobbes expressed his version of this theory. In *Leviathan*, Hobbes argued that dissension and conflict are inevitable, that society is made "civil" by tacit agreement—a "social contract"—allowing rulers to resolve or contain conflicts. The Hobbesian model was a naturalist theory of political order; no appeal to divinity was made.

Justice Holmes saw the competition of interests as inevitable; he thought people would either submit to law or kill one another. Therefore it was a judge's duty to recognize and even facilitate conflict, while also restraining it. As a judge, Holmes said, he would "help people go to Hell if they wished," so long as they did so in lawful ways. This posture gave Holmes's writing a "progressive" cast. He could side with the underdog—a labor union or dissident group—which was beleaguered and difficult to defend. Holmes did not necessarily support these causes, but he thought they should be treated as legitimate interests and that conflict should go forward without predetermining who should win or what policies should prevail.

In the early twentieth century, when new voices were struggling to be heard, Holmes seemed to be a principled supporter of organized labor and free speech. But he saw freedom of speech and association as only *presumptively* beneficial. The conflict of interests was a social good, although subject to rules protecting public order and safety.

A somewhat different philosophy views social life as cooperative and resourceful. In this view, government is more facilitative than controlling, more committed to valued ways of life than to preventing strife.

Government is not (mostly) neutral among contending interests. It may recognize, for example, that racism is not "just another interest" but a threat to communal well-being.

The doctrines of Hobbes and Holmes resonate strongly with pluralist ideas, which check power with countervailing power. Social history is indeed a history of struggle, but some struggles are more tolerable than others, if they pursue their aims in accord with the norms of civilized society.

Common-law judging is a largely *cognitive* enterprise. The judges are supposed to know how social relations emerge and what happens to them as circumstances change. Until the end of the nineteenth century, for example, a contract of employment was assumed to be "at will," meaning that an employee could quit or be dismissed without notice or compensation. This "at will" doctrine did not take account of the realities of modern industry, and in time the courts came to see that, at least for "regular" employees, the discretion of employers was not absolute. The new doctrine made law more sensitive to social facts and more responsive to legitimate interests.

Since the eighteenth century, government has been downgraded as a source of order and creativity. Society, not government, is the main and best source of energy, cooperation, and responsibility. This view was expressed by Thomas Paine:

[Social order] has its origin in the principles of society and in the natural constitution of man. It existed prior to government and would exist if the formality of government was abolished. The mutual dependence and reciprocal interest which a man has upon man, and all the parts of a civilized community have upon each other, create that great chain of connection which holds it together. Common interest regulates their concerns and forms their law, and the laws which common usage ordains have a greater influence than the laws of government.[4]

Paine helped formulate the emerging ideology of commercial and industrial capitalism: society is largely *self-regulating*; order and responsibility arise from cooperation and self-interest.

These and similar views led to new goals and policies. Law and government would establish order and protect ordinary pursuits. An *informed* sensibility, not order imposed by Leviathan, should prevail. Law should be fashioned from and contribute to the realization of legitimate expectations; it would find and clarify the foundations of well-being in domestic, economic, and political institutions. Common-law judges would then be *analysts* as well as oracles.

Law in Context

In the social science of law, the phrase "law in context" refers to the many ways legal ideas and institutions are affected by an ambient cultural and social matrix. Legal ideas are animated and transformed by what Holmes called the "felt necessities" of a time and place. Law is in and of society, adapting to its contours, giving direction to change. Therefore, blurred boundaries—between law and morality, law and politics, law and economics, law and custom—are signs of good order.

Legal institutions need public confidence and support. In a well-functioning legal system, the decisions of judges and legislators make sense to those whose rights and obligations are affected. However, the blurring of *boundaries* does not mean that *distinctions* between law and other social spheres—morality, custom, politics—can be ignored. Law says which norms are *binding* and will be enforced. Other obligations stem from kinship, ownership, subordination, and cooperation, not from courts and legislatures.

The interdependence of law and society is revealed in the legal recognition of custom. Law is most readily obeyed when it is rooted in and justified by a community's moral and constitutional heritage. In the late eighteenth century, the rebellious American colonies sought rights justified more by historical entitlements than by political or moral theory. They demanded "the rights of Englishmen."

Although legal *rules* are necessarily tailored to kinds of activities, legal *principles* derive from more general values and from the lessons of experience. What constitutes a binding contract depends on expressed or implied agreement. In cases of negligence, the rules reflect socially recognized standards of care, that is, shared ideas about personal or institutional responsibility. What it means to be responsible is only partly determined by a particular context, such as building a house. These contexts bring into play assumptions about rationality and commitment, and these assumptions transcend cultural or institutional contexts.

In indentifying human rights, law takes account of *basic* needs and sufferings. Wherever people are subject to heavy constraints (or close supervision), questions of limits and empathy are raised. Disrespectful and degrading practices violate human rights, and oppression hinders creativity and saps initiative. Prisoners, students, soldiers, ordinary employees are all more likely to obey rules, and be better at what they do, if they are treated with concern for their physical and emotional needs. There is no wall of separation between such principles and fidelity to context. Principles of care, reciprocity, and responsibility are applied in the light of what a particular relationship or activity possibly requires and are upheld while taking into account the context, whether it is manufacturing products, interrogating prisoners, or managing a classroom. These obligations call for knowledge of what it means to be fair, loyal, and cooperative; the standards reflect realistic assessments of what makes for effectiveness. Each setting is to some extent unique and has its own needs and constraints, a reminder that the application of principles is not a purely logical process.

The study of law "in context" moves analysis from abstraction to concreteness. For example, the blameworthiness of an offender, or the responsibility of a principal for harms caused by an agent, takes account of *particular* facts regarding conditions and options. Law is more effective, and more just, when it is context-sensitive or "individualized." Contextual thinking is a way of realizing moral ideals.

Law in Action

Another theme in the science of justice is the injunction to study "law in action." A legal order consists of agencies that, like other legal actors, live in dynamic social worlds. Social scientists have described how legal systems work: how burdensome caseloads are handled, how rough justice is dispensed, how ideals of equality or rehabilitation are affected by the realities of policing and detention. None of this is surprising to students of organization, who have long recognized the difference between "formal" and "informal," or "operative," procedures. The operative system reflects situational pressures, temptations, and outlooks.

Much of social science makes plain what social systems are really like, including how they deviate from stated forms or purposes. This counterposition of ideals and realities reveals the truth—a humanist truth—that everyday life is concrete, not abstract, governed significantly by the self-regarding needs of persons and groups.

Law in action strikes an *antiformalist* note, but ideals and standards are not ignored. On the contrary, their fragility is made plain.

Natural Law

The perspective sketched above has much in common with the natural-law tradition in jurisprudence and moral philosophy, yet it departs from that tradition in important ways. The natural-law tradition, best understood as the philosophy and science of justice,[5] holds that law, morality, and social knowledge are interdependent. This interdependence is a challenge to "legal positivism," which insists on a sharp separation of law and morality and associates law with sovereign will, divine or secular, democratic or authoritarian. Natural-law jurisprudence traces legal authority to reason rather than will. The authority of reason derives from purportedly sound knowledge of human nature and collective life. This is a troubling doctrine for those who see God's commandments as the book of law. The dissonance is overcome, in part at least, by associating divine will with justice and good order. God is a humanist deity, mindful of human needs, impulses, strength, and weakness.

In natural-law jurisprudence, law is subordinated to justice by claiming divine sanction for legal principles, such as respect for equal humanity of all subjects, including criminals. God unites power and perfection, reason and will. The study and worship of God rest on confidence that His will is just and mindful, not arbitrary or indifferent.

In the life of reason, inquiry knows no near stopping place. Reason calls for sustained study of the human condition, especially our *spiritual* well-being. When Saint Thomas Aquinas defined law as "an ordinance of reason for the common good," he took the common good to be mainly spiritual rather than material prosperity or military might. Because rulers have a duty to discover this good, they must look to knowledge for guidance. They thereby bridge the gap between reason and will. Natural-law jurisprudence obeys a dual imperative: to vindicate morality and to do so in the light of sound knowledge. These imperatives bind law to ideals, and to science too.

If "experience" is the "life of the law," as Oliver Wendell Holmes, Jr., once wrote, a science of justice is needed to draw lessons from experience, to learn what enhances or degrades the human capacity to live well and not merely survive.

Something more than deductive reasoning is needed; empirical study of what works and at what cost is essential. For example, it cannot be deduced from the idea of government whether a government has "sovereign immunity" (barring suits against it without its consent). In fact, rulers do bind themselves by rules that they can change as they wish; they respect their own rules because it is convenient to do so. We need to know when and how such self-restraint occurs, and empirical study will reveal the pertinent variables. Such findings are conditional, probabilistic, and subject to correction. In short, natural-law jurisprudence as a secular philosophy tests law by its findings about power and society. Thus social knowledge, though uncertain and controversial, has legal authority. Ideas about opportunity, motivation, intent, and care are based on history, psychology, sociology, and economics. This matrix of authoritative ideas, respected by lawyers and judges, makes law less certain but more realistic and just. Legal certainty is at risk because justice is founded on knowledge.

A natural-law jurisprudence relies on inquiry and argument, not on unquestioned authority. This is the difference between modern natural-law jurisprudence and earlier versions that were more closely bound to theology.

Part Three   Philosophy and Social Science

10

Moral Philosophy and Social Science

A PERSISTENT SUBTEXT of the preceding chapters is the interdependence and complementarity of social science and moral philosophy. Philosophy analyzes ideas and purported fundamental attributes of the self; social science studies varieties, contexts, and enabling or disabling conditions. These efforts often overlap. Hobbes, Descartes, Hume, Rousseau, Kant, and Hegel drew on history as well moral and political experience. Their work was enhanced by logical argument and persuasive rhetoric. For Hobbes, speculative reasoning is badly flawed without factual data on how values emerge, are sustained, or are displaced. Moreover, social life comes in many varieties, and each should be understood in the light of its own circumstances.

Max Weber (1864–1920) wrote masterfully about rationality, bureaucracy, religion, and law, and he relied on history for his conclusions about intellectual and institutional trends and brought to his work a mind alert to kinds and contexts. This helped blur the line between history and social science. Interpretation, he argued, must be disciplined by factual knowledge. His best-known work, *The Protestant Ethic and the Spirit of Capitalism*, combined philosophical and theological sophistication with historical analysis. This was a way of giving direction and relevance to social inquiry. Substituting *theory* for *philosophy*, he connected ideas to historical facts about politics, economics, and religions. He did so by identifying *kinds* of belief, solidarity, and conflict.

A similar transition from philosophy to social science marks the work of Emile Durkheim (1858–1917). In his studies of the division of labor and suicide rates, Durkheim turned the philosophy of history into a science of society. He studied kinds of cohesion implicit in division of labor and accounted for observed differences in suicide rates among well-integrated and relatively unattached populations. Durkheim's writings heralded a shift away from ungrounded speculation in favor of factual inquiries about isolation and alienation. What made Durkheim a *theorist* was his gift for abstraction and his perception of trends; what made him a *sociologist* was his attention to social relations.

Naturalism in Ethics

The special contribution of social science to moral theory is its affirmation of a naturalist ethic. The ancient Greek philosophers, as we have seen, had confidence in human will and reason, a confidence that was renewed by later thinkers who saw reason in nature. Aquinas, Machiavelli, Bacon, Spinoza, and Hobbes found reason in the mind of man as well as in the will and wisdom of God. Philosophers were encouraged to rely on their own powers of analysis and imagination. They invented new ideas, such as "social contract," which grounded legitimacy in the consent of the governed. The triumph of secular over religious thought was an aspect of "enlightenment." These early-modern thinkers drew lessons for mankind from currents of history. Philosophers became heroes, and prophets as well. They anticipated the contributions of social science to moral inquiry, but only dimly perceived the benefits of empirical observation. Their style was dogmatic and polemical rather than self-critical and self-correcting. Yet they made way for (and contributed to) more disciplined thought about social life. Hence the history of social thought has been and remains a necessary part of the education of social scientists.

High on the agenda of the emerging social science was a concept of "nature" more general than that of physics and biology. A natural order is to be discerned in the persistent and recurrent forms of social life; morality is not something alien or imposed.

The Ontogeny of Ideals

A prominent theme in moral conduct is the discipline of ideals and standards. Many norms arise, *without design*, as criteria of success or failure. "Nature" is what people learn about cooking, cleaning, child rearing, and animal husbandry. This "nature" is revealed in recurrent facts about political, economic, educational, religious, and family experience—realities that lead to success or failure, satisfaction or frustration. Ideals are not brought to mankind as Promethean fire stolen from the gods; they arise from the satisfactions and disappointments that come from following or amending a nature that sets limits and affords opportunities.

A basic teaching of humanist pragmatism is *learning from experience*. Humans flourish when their identities are formed by kinship, locality, and belief. These particular connections generate the diversity that modern anthropology has emphasized. The primacy of the particular also upholds the "psychic unity" of mankind. Humans are One as well as Many: the benefits and burdens of particularity are *universal* human experience. The diversity of cultures is plain, but so is the psychic unity manifested in feelings of pride and affection. Anthropology teaches that all peoples have much the same biological capacities and limits. As the commonalities show, despite diversity, cultures are *human* products.

Anthropological theorists have identified many "universals," such as kinship, hospitality, and much else. The universals allow for variety in form and meaning. This theory lessens the significance of diversity by attending to the recurrence of similar problems and solutions. The focus shifts from particular practices to more general functions.

This point was made by Alexander Goldenweiser, an anthropologist who noted that, in all societies, many widely practiced activities, such as hunting, fishing, and gardening, depend for success on effective adaptation of means and ends. Good choices are based on sound knowledge of what makes for a good boat or a successful transmission of crafts and rituals. People learn to fashion an oar that pulls well and shelters that weather storms. The differences are limited by what humans can do, by the physics of floatation, and by the realities of stormy weather.

Objectivity and Well-Being

A theory of morality asks, What is the truth-value of assertions about "the good"? Is there an objective criterion? Or is "good" an expression of what has been called the "naturalistic fallacy"? Many normative judgments are indeed subjective expressions of preferences. Others, however, *evaluate* preferences, as when we say eating whole grains is a healthy dietary choice, regardless of preference. We may be able to say what makes a burglar successful without necessarily endorsing his actions. Every context, or kind of context, has distinctive needs and resources. The moral and psychological health of a child depends on objective standards of nurture and instruction, and for that there must be knowledge as well as resolve.

Here is the model for social science as moral inquiry. Goodness is a condition, known by its contribution to survival and flourishing. Determining the well-being of an administrative system is an important concern of political science; in psychology, emotional health; in economics, free markets; in sociology, the morale and cohesion of social systems.

Social scientists sometimes use the concept of "function" to analyze coherence and conflict. Social arrangements are said to be "functional" or "dysfunctional." This idiom presumes that we can know objectively what sustains or limits unity or competence of a social system, for example, an effective or disruptive form of communication or supervision.

The jewel in the crown of philosophical inquiry is justification by reason. Argument, not faith; analysis, not tradition; autonomy, not subservience—these are the true indicators of moral well-being in government, religion, or education. However, the meaning of reason is not self-evident. Is it logic? Rhetoric? Thought based on observation and evidence?

In intellectual history, reason combines facts with arguments, as in theories of the quality of consent in political communities. Experience is invoked, as when Rousseau said: "Man is born free but is everywhere in bondage."[1] This famous remark is not undisciplined speculation. It draws moral lessons from recurrent facts about obedience, self-interest, and authority. The perils of governance are studied, and those inquiries form a social science of political life.

Deontology and Consequentialism

A naturalist ethic speaks to (and amends) a familiar argument in moral philosophy. A deontological ethic is *duty*-centered or *rights*-centered. The Mosaic Code or Ten Commandments invokes divine will and wisdom; the pious motto is *Thy* will be done. In contrast, a consequentialist ethic considers the *effects* of pride, deceit, violence, theft, and covetous desire. A naturalist ethic asks: Consequences for what? Deontology speaks to the character of a person, institution, or game. Following set rules upholds standards that make games like poker, chess, or bridge coherent and satisfying. Without respect for rules, the game becomes confusing and disorderly. Deontological rules spell out what it means to be a good citizen or soldier, a devout Christian or Muslim. Each honors fidelity and is vulnerable to characteristic temptations. For deontology, the relevant consequences are those that sustain or harm an ongoing perspective, relationship, or activity.

The difference between deontology and consequentialism is that between *internal* and *external* effects—that is, between maintaining the character or coherence of an enterprise and affecting an outcome.

Moral Well-Being

Coherence and consistency are ingredients of integrity. For moral well-being, there must also be concern for values or functions. Integrity entails soundness as well as coherence, a duality that we find in the circulatory system of an animal and the plumbing of a house. Each system is said to work badly when it delivers the wrong fluids or delivers the right fluids at the wrong time.

The main criterion is moral competence, that is, the disposition and capacity to engage in other-regarding conduct. These virtues form a personal or institutional "character." The capacity of a business to make moral choices in its dealings with employees, customers, competitors, investors, and government is a prominent theme in the study of corporate decision making. To have the care of a person or institution is to be responsible for its character, not only for its narrowly defined goals. Moral well-being is not a "pie in the sky" concept. It needs skills and resources that make moral choices easy and rewarding.

A deontological ethic has a mainly *internal* relevance. The state of the system is at the forefront of strategic thinking. A marginal firm in a highly competitive industry may lack the resources needed for virtue, or even survival.

That moral competence needs congenial conditions provides a gateway to social science, which then is a kind of moral inquiry. Sober realism, not wishful thinking, is the guide. It cannot be assumed that good intentions prevail. Instead, empirical analysis examines how parochial interests trump the common good.

Moral Experience

The primary datum of a naturalist ethic is moral experience—that is, the way in which people realize ideals and limit self-regard. The outcome is not purity, because moral experience responds to conflicting impulses and divergent pressures. A moral order derives shape and texture from challenges and opportunities.

The Kantian "categorical imperative"—act according to a principle that every rational being should follow—supports a *universalist* morality. This may include special loyalties to kin, friends, coreligionists, fellow countrymen. In Kant's philosophy, rationality is the foundation of morality, and Kant was right to see that moral claims must be universalizable even when they refer to parochial interests. Universalizability refers to the *logic* of morality, as in the connection between morality and other-regarding attitudes. The morality of parenting derives from reproduction and intimate association—that is, from particular experiences, not from an abstract logic of moral obligation. A prohibition against making false promises is necessary for social order, but that conclusion requires support of relevant *facts*, not logic alone. By itself, the concept of rationality will not tell us which norms best advance a specific purpose or a special competence.

Moreover, a *universalizable* norm is not necessarily *universal*. A universal norm transcends local attachments; it may express concern for general human needs and potentialities. Universal (or "universalist") norms posit a common humanity and warrant treatment of all people with concern and respect. This reality engenders obligations, which should be examined empirically, in the light of what people owe one another. These obligations arise in contexts that produce benefits, constraints, and opportunities among parents, siblings, colleagues, and citizens.

The morality of governance was addressed in the *Federalist Papers*,[2] where the principle of "checks and balances" was invoked to make government less dangerous and more responsive. A primary concern is the coherence and competence—the *integrity*—of persons, activities, and institutions. When integrity is weakened, an inner strength is lost, especially the ability to adapt to new circumstances without loss of purpose or corruption of values. Integrity is protected by restraints on official conduct. Thus, it is wrong to counterpose deontology and consequentialism. A deontological ethic does consider consequences, such as the effects of a belief or a course of conduct on character or integrity.

Much moral experience has to do with meeting personal or professional standards. For example, the moral promise of a family dinner stems from the values it can realize, such as solidarity, relaxation, and intimacy. Although often incompletely realized, these ideals are vital guides to purpose and cooperation. Of course, not every standard is a moral ideal. Moral ideals emerge when self-respect and fellowship are in play—that is, when good-faith effort and concern for others are animating principles. The driver of an automobile is reckless and negligent if he fails to meet standards of care and self-control. The standards are moral insofar as they uphold responsible conduct.

Even incompletely realized ideals may be part of moral experience. Standards are variably embraced or ignored; therefore empirical study of how choices are made is required. The realization of ideals is often limited by competition with other values and commitments, such as loyalty. As ideals encounter one another, the line between moral philosophy and social science becomes unclear.

In a theological perspective, evil is natural and prevalent. Its main source is egotism, which appears in many guises. The chief casualty is social responsibility. A recurrent drama is enacted that upholds the legitimacy of self-interest and responsibility. Because evil is so often inextricably mixed with the good, it must be *checked*, rather than eradicated. This is not a purist strategy, for it goes hand in hand with appreciating the worth of self-regard.

Deliberation plays a leading part in moral judgment, identifying appropriate ways of making decisions when the values at stake are disputed or unclear. Especially important is to say what has *intrinsic* worth and therefore can be a starting point for moral reasoning.

Bounded Subjectivity

Naturalism in ethics is a voice of resistance to subjectivist inclinations in social theory and moral philosophy. Some theorists have supposed that human minds are powerful and vulnerable, active as well as receptive. Such ideas raise man up by giving his mind a creative role in history.

In Plato's parable of the cave (see Chapter 1), men discern only shadows of their ambient worlds. In the late eighteenth century, Kant argued for the epistemological creativity of the knowing subject. A world of *appearances* gains clarity from categories imposed by the human mind, such as space, time, and causality. These and similar conjectures endow humankind with crucial powers. People see their worlds in their own ways and are also shaped by their creations. *Consciousness* forms the world and is in turn formed by it. In this view, human history is mainly a history of consciousness—of awareness, perception, and belief. With apologies to Emerson, we might say: "Ideas are in the saddle and ride mankind."

Social science has taken the same tack, with sails more tautly trimmed. Rejecting generalities about mind and history, it turns to more focused and more empirical analysis of consciousness, including its causes and effects.

A major transitional figure was Karl Marx, who traced working-class consciousness to the disciplines and solidarities of capitalist "relations of production." Marx saw these experiences as sources of *class* consciousness and *socialist* sensibility. He gave great weight to the *objective conditions* of factory work, as determinants of *subjective* responses, thus combining a Hegelian philosophy of history with a more focused interpretation of working-class life. In this he anticipated a twentieth-century social science study, *Management and the Worker*,[3] which examined the unauthorized but effective control of production in a factory setting. These findings are in tune with Marxist theory, without accepting his generalizations about history, consciousness, and the inevitability of socialism.

Another relevant theorist is George Herbert Mead (1863–1931), who studied the consciousness of children in families and peer groups. Mead distinguished the "significant other" of intimate association from the "generalized other" of culture, religion, and political affiliation. He argued that through participation in games and other activities children learn the rules and premises of social life. Unlike Marx, Mead saw consciousness as producing cohesion rather than conflict or alienation. Marx and Mead noticed different facets of consciousness, yet both stressed the importance of knowing its varieties and contexts. They analyzed the interactions that give intensity and direction to social life. In this way, philosophy of history is made relevant to social science.

11

A Public Philosophy

IN PART TWO, "Realms of Value," I argued that major disciplines in social science are importantly value-centered, much concerned with ideals realized, weakened, or displaced. Rationality in organization, democracy in government, impartiality in justice are not mere preferences—they are values summoned and sustained by knowable imperatives. Each setting has its own criteria of well-being and success; each benefits from empirical study of both facts and values. To know the special spheres and standards of government, education, business, and religion is a chief aim of social science. A related goal is to enhance public morality by identifying truths—derived from and supported by the findings of social science—that should be accepted as learned wisdom, or a "public philosophy."

A "public philosophy" speaks to matters of public concern and serves as a source of insight and judgment. It consists of generalizations about persons, groups, and institutions that justify expectations and warn of dangers. Examples are Lord Acton's dictum that "power corrupts and absolute power corrupts absolutely," Charles Merriam's concept of the "poverty of power," and James Madison's doctrine that good government calls for "checks and balances." Such generalizations say what we can *rely upon* and what we must *guard against*. They challenge social science to focus on what Max Weber called the "value-relevance" (*Wertbeziehung*) of social facts. They represent people *as they are* and *as they can be*. The well-being of a person or an institution depends upon that person's or institution's special needs being met and its special circumstances being understood.

In this chapter I examine some major strands of public philosophy.

Freedom and Human Nature

In 1776 the signers of the Declaration of Independence held "these truths to be self-evident: that all men are created equal; that they are endowed by their Creator with certain unalienable rights; that among these rights are life, liberty, and the pursuit of happiness." This doctrine is an implicit theory of human nature, expressed in terms of the pious religion of the age. It says intrusive controls should be curbed or eliminated and subordinates of all kinds should be treated with respect as autonomous beings. The implicit ideal of personal freedom is upheld. The enemy of freedom is regimentation. For example, close-order drill is much favored in military circles, but it is not a good model for social life, cooperation, and obedience.

Rights—and the freedoms they protect—are limited by common purposes and by the rights of others. Such limits are set by the requirements of cohesion and coordination. In a landmark case having to do with this issue, for example,[1] the U.S. Supreme Court upheld a married couple's right to use contraceptives during sexual intercourse. The Court found a "right of privacy" in American constitutional law, and this right protected the freedom of married couples to block biological effects of intimate sexual activity. "Privacy" is a bundle of mostly unspecified personal choices, such as where to live, whether, when, and whom to marry, whether to reproduce and how many children to have, what vocation or religion to adopt. Such choices create new responsibilities—of spouses to one another, of parents to children. These obligations are mainly self-chosen, and they create and uphold a social fabric. Thus understood, the "pursuit of happiness" is a defense of self-interest.

Kinship and Identity

No finding of social science is more firmly grounded than the human disposition to form distinctive identities. In the construction of selves, "I" and "we" are closely connected, sustained by feelings of belonging, the gratifications of relatedness, and interaction. Organizations of all kinds rely on such gratification for initiative and morale. The interplay of selfhood and participation has mostly welcome effects. It has moral significance in that it creates objects of care and concern. This idea is a mainstay of cultural anthropology, which respects diverse ways of life and a positive attitude toward ordinary life experience. The *particularity* of social experience points to the moral worth in individuality. We discern strength and weakness in modes of interaction. This perspective helps us to know what humanity means and what its affirmation requires.

Beyond Individualism

The wish to escape close supervision is a well-known response in social life. This principle of "good human relations"—subject to norms of accountability—is a frequent source of moral ambiguity. That freedom is necessary for creativity, initiative, and willing cooperation is a stumbling block for advocates of "tough" administration.

The doctrine of individualism prizes initiative, competition, and taking advantage of opportunity. Short shrift is given to the full range of affected interests and to the contributions of apparently unrelated circumstances. Society is thought of as populated by heroes who take risks and accept responsibilities in the course of pursuing their special interests. The need for cooperation and subordination is slighted.

The alternative recognizes the importance of collective contributions. Individualism upholds the intrinsic worth of human persons, but has a narrowed understanding of that worth. Interdependence is in fact inescapable and mostly beneficial. It is a large part of what social science is about, since it encourages study of contexts to determine the kinds of freedom or subordination appropriate to the particular context. The interdependence of human activities presents a high barrier for individualism. Social institutions depend on cooperation and solidarity; what people achieve is seldom due only to their own efforts.

This is not an argument against higher rewards for greater contributions. It does suggest, however, that collective contributions should be recognized as such and that differences in compensation and privilege are not inevitable.

Nurture and Discipline

According to the Christian gospel, Jesus said, "Love one another." This principle endows each person with inherent worth and also assumes that each depends on relatives, friends, and others for emotional and practical help. This attitude is compatible with "tough" or "responsible" love, where control carries with it responsibility for nurture, as in child rearing. Individual circumstances as a general principle are invoked. Discipline is often necessary for nurture, especially in teaching and parenting.

Studies of moral development have examined fidelity to abstract ideals such as fairness. However, a "different voice" takes its departure from the concreteness of persons, groups, and beliefs and honors virtues of caring and commitment.[2] Moral development is seen as an enlarged capacity to experience empathy and show concern. The object of concern is a particular person, group, doctrine, or activity. The "law of love" commands respect for the wholeness and uniqueness of fellow humans. Moral development, as the psychic capacity to make commitments and recognize needs, is not exclusively abstract or concrete. Doing justice or achieving moral competence is necessarily partly cognitive and abstract, as the meanings of responsibility and caring must be grasped. Commitment to particular others is diminished when people are thought of as interchangeable or fungible, and abstract formulations ignore or override the welfare of specific persons or groups.[3]

Pluralism and Civil Society

Pluralist ideas argue for the interdependence of society and government. Society is composed of many kinds of groups, which differ in function, capability, and intrinsic worth. Conflict among these groups is not unwanted "noise." Rather, it is a benign disorder, opposing power to power in an open society. Participatory pluralism encourages groups to influence policies that matter to them. Government is made more responsive and also more vulnerable. Some groups are likely to get special attention and deference. This vulnerability is the great peril of responsiveness and is sometimes called the "capture" of public agencies by parochial interests.

Pluralist doctrines are necessary resources for good government. Democracy is strengthened when new voices can be heard, although the same voices may distort decisions by protecting some interests and neglecting others. Although responsiveness is a worthy ideal, its course must be monitored and controlled. Here again, empirical study is guided by normative concerns.

James Madison invoked pluralist ideas when he wrote: "Ambition must be made to counteract ambition. . . . The constant aim is to divide and arrange the several offices in such manner as that each may be a check on the other—that the private interest of every individual may be a sentinel over the public rights."[4]

Pluralism is a chief component of liberal thought, which sees the social world as composed of multiple and contending interests, each capable of making its voice heard and all strong enough to form coalitions and limit the power of opponents, including government agencies.

The Primacy of Civil Society

It is a premise of pluralism that effective government requires a flourishing civil society. This premise was reinforced by the traumas of the twentieth century. Nazi and Communist totalitarianism sought to crush autonomous groups, demanding full support for an all-powerful, all-encompassing party-state. In response, "civil society" became a watch-word for opponents of totalitarian rule.

The concept of civil society resonates strongly with pluralist theory. What we prize in community is a unity that preserves the integrity of the constituent parts. Private groups are protected from centralized power, individuals from isolation and moral disarray.

Civil society fosters autonomy and respects diversity, reciprocity, interdependence, and other groups. Rights are not *gifts* of government but are recognized and protected by it.

Thomas Paine invoked this idea when he wrote:

> Government is no farther necessary than to supply the few cases to which society and civilization are not conveniently competent; and instances are not wanting to show, that everything which government can usefully add thereto, has been performed by the common consent of society, without government.[5]

Paine's theory was anticipated by John Locke, who emphasized the difference between a *constructed* community governed by human will and an *undesigned, self-regulating* community governed by natural law. The constructed community is derivative, not constitutive. It presumes a moral order but does not create one. In Locke's thought, a constructed community is founded upon consent and its authority is limited by the purposes for which consent is given. Therefore government should be *counterposed* to the society that created it and to which it is accountable. The prosperity and good order of society is the test of good government. In short, civil society has moral primacy.

The primacy of civil society does not, however, save it from critical assessments of its capacity to enhance participation and curb abuses of power. Left to itself, civil society subordinates the common good to private interests. Its main function is to limit government and enhance the moral competence of private associations.

I have elsewhere[6] suggested that "core" participation occurs when membership in large, relatively impersonal associations or communities is mediated by membership in person-centered groups. It brings the energies and incentives of intimate association to impersonal settings. A government hostile to civil society is likely to be inhumane and disabled.

Ideals Without Illusions

Moral realism is the centerpiece of Reinhold Niebuhr's analysis of "irony" in human history. An ironic view is appropriate when illusion or pretense obscures the true nature of collective decision. Niebuhr argues that we should recognize a pervasive human temptation to deny these facts by pretending that they are not necessary or relevant. The denial upholds a governing ideal, but does so without acknowledging (or evaluating) hard choices. The moral element is the authority of the ideal; realism appears in strategies that take account of human frailty and temptation. This theory traces illusion to human nature and the nature of politics; the correction is humility and self-scrutiny.

Niebuhr drew on biblical interpretations, but similar conclusions are supported by the findings of political science, sociology, and psychology. The lesson is that ideals cannot be realized without protecting them from illusions. Democracy is a *corruptible* form of self-government, often marred by demagogy and flawed representation. Social science studies these potentials for corruption and tries to devise alternatives.

President John F. Kennedy once said of himself that he was "an idealist without illusions."[7] The strands of public philosophy discussed in this chapter share a poignant premise: any activity can have unintended and unwanted effects. This theme has a theological corollary: only God displays a union of power and perfection. For humans, who live in worlds of contingency and contradiction, power and perfection are necessarily at odds.

To avoid such outcomes, unintended effects are acknowledged and contained.

The Debasement of Ideals

"Debasement" is a moral judgment that should be founded on inquiry that combines empirical observation with contexts and clarified by philosophical analysis of the values at risk. Ideals are tarnished by the means used to achieve them. Thus, evil is done in the name of good. To bridge the gap between ideals and outcomes, the strengths and weaknesses of social arrangements must be brought out. This is done by discerning the conditions that produce healthy or pathological states.

A relevant contribution of social science is Robert Michels's landmark study of European social democracy. Michels argued that nominally democratic organizations are subject to an "iron law of oligarchy." "Who says organization," he wrote, "says oligarchy."

Michels had little confidence in the realization of ideals. "The socialists may conquer, but not socialism." He closed the Italian edition of his book (1962), with a memorable passage:

The democratic currents of history resemble successive waves. They break ever on the same shoals. They are ever renewed. . . . When democracies have gained a certain stage of development, they undergo a gradual transformation, adopting the aristocratic spirit, and in many cases also the aristocratic forms, against which at the outset they struggled so fiercely. . . . It is probable that this cruel game will continue without end.[8]

This bleak conclusion misreads the moral lesson we should take from Michels's work. Better to read him as revealing a process that prevails *in the absence of countervailing measures*. The process Michels discerned is real enough, rooted in ever-present incentives and imperatives. This is his lasting contribution. However, the appropriate response is *intelligent design*, not despair. We do not, however, reject Michels, for we accept the truth in his theory.

We should also address another inevitable risk: the contingency of policy and choice. Any social fabric has a rough and uneven texture, for it is the product of many particular decisions and events, of roads not taken or only tentatively explored, of opportunities missed, limits recognized or ignored. These contingencies invite inquiry into the ways ideals are affected by congenial or uncongenial conditions. Moral realism does not shrink from the ironies and frustrations of collective action, for it combines awareness with resolve—that is, with a determination to curb and redirect pernicious tendencies.

Contingency and Ambiguity

A well-known theory in social psychology holds that toleration of ambiguity is a healthy defense against ideas that oversimplify the world and harden differences. The alternative is the will and capacity to accept ambiguities. This ironic attitude is more than a mode of self-expression. Ambiguous outcomes are thought of as challenges to rational choice.

THE TEACHINGS I HAVE DISCUSSED ABOVE are supported by political, economic, and sociological science. Normative as well as descriptive, they say what should be done or anticipated in the light of recurrent experience. Contingency and ambiguity are contained, not eliminated.

In this chapter I have analyzed some themes in the public philosophy of social science, stressing the prevalence of ambiguity and contingency. The right response, sometimes called wisdom, accepts reality and does not deny or evade it. In this philosophy, *integrity* is a centerpiece—the ability to know and the will to meet challenges set by disputed goals and changing circumstances. What is sought is an equilibrium that is realistic about illusions' holding fast to self-defining principles.

Notes

Foreword

1. *The Moral Commonwealth* (Berkeley: University of California Press, 1992), x.
2. "Jurisprudence and Social Policy: Aspirations and Perspectives," *California Law Review* 68 (1980): 208.
3. *The Moral Commonwealth*, xii.
4. See "Tribute to Amitai Etzioni by Philip Selznick," 11th Annual Meeting on Socio-Economics, Madison, Wisconsin, July 9, 1999, http://www.sase.org/conf1999/selznick.html.
5. Donald Black, review of *Law, Society, and Industrial Justice*, in *American Journal of Sociology* 78 (1972): 709–714.
6. Philip Selznick, reply to Black's review, *American Journal of Sociology* 78 (1973): 1266–1269.

Chapter 1

1. In the tradition of ancient Greece, the motto "Know thyself" was inscribed on the Oracle of Apollo at Delphi.
2. See Benjamin Jowett, *The Dialogues of Plato*, vol. 1 (New York: Random House, 1937), 420.
3. Plato made this point in his "Parable of the Cave." See *The Republic*, book 7.
4. This is the sentence inscribed around the interior dome of the Jefferson Memorial in Washington, D.C. The quote was taken from a letter to Dr. Benjamin Rush, September 23, 1800.
5. Jean Jacques Rousseau, *The Social Contract* (Chicago: Regnery, 1954), 2.
6. Enlightenment humanism should include some technically pre-Enlightenment figures of the sixteenth and seventeenth centuries, such as Hobbes, Descartes, Locke, and Spinoza, and early scientists like Galileo.
7. From the poem "Pied Beauty" by Gerard Manley Hopkins.
8. See Thomas M. Raysor, *Coleridge's Shakespearean Criticism*, vol. 1 (Cambridge, Mass.: Harvard University Press, 1930), 224.

9. See Immanuel Kant, *Foundations of the Metaphysics of Morals* (Indianapolis: Bobbs-Merrill, 1969), 52.

10. See Karl Marx, *Economic and Philosophical Manuscripts* (New York: International Publishers, 1980), 292.

11. See Leonard Krieger, *Ranke: The Meaning of History* (Chicago: University of Chicago Press, 1977), 4.

Chapter 2

1. Dennis Wrong, "The Oversocialized Conception of Man in Modern Society," *American Sociological Review* 26 (1961): 183–193.

2. For German-speakers, this transition was easy to make, given the connotations of *Geist* and *geistigkeit*.

3. Sir Henry Sumner Maine, in *Ancient Law* (Boston: Beacon, 1963), 163.

4. James B. Conant, *Science and Common Sense* (New Haven: Yale University Press, 1964), 58–59.

5. John Dewey, *Experience and Nature* (New York: Dover, 1958), 51.

6. J. W. N. Watkins, "Historical Explanations in the Social Sciences," *British Journal for the Philosophy of Science* 8 (1957): 105–106.

Chapter 3

1. John Stuart Mill, *Utilitarianism* (London: J. M. Dent and Sons, 1944), 10–11.

2. George A. Schrader, "Autonomy, Heteronomy, and Moral Imperatives," in *I. Kant: Foundations of the Metaphysics of Morals with Critical Essays* (Indianapolis: Bobbs-Merrill Educational Publishing, 1969).

3. See Max Weber, "Politics as Vocation" in *From Max Weber: Essays in Sociology*, trans. and ed. H. H. Gerth and C. Wright Mills (New York: Oxford University Press, 1946), 77–128.

4. Max Weber, "Objectivity in Social Science," in *The Methodology of the Social Sciences*, ed. E. A. Shils and H. A. Finch (Glencoe, Ill.: Free Press, 1949).

5. Leo Strauss, "Natural Right and the Distinction Between Facts and Values," in *Natural Right and History* (Chicago: University of Chicago Press, 1953), 53.

6. John Dewey, "Anti-Naturalism in Extremis," *Partisan Review* 10 (1943): 32.

7. George Santayana, *The Life of Reason* (1933; reprint, New York: Scribner's, 1954), 102.

Chapter 4

1. See David Gauthier, *Morals by Agreement* (Oxford: Clarendon, 1986).

2. Hannah Arendt, *The Origins of Totalitarianism* (New York: Harcourt, Brace, 1951), 294.

3. Subsidiarity is the doctrine, associated with Catholic social theory, holding that

the constituent parts of a larger unity are entitled to respect and to some measure of autonomy. This doctrine is closely connected to the idea of federalism.

4. Thomas Hobbes, *Leviathan* (1651; reprint, London: Pelican, 1968), 375.

5. Lon L. Fuller, *The Morality of Law* (New Haven: Yale University Press, 1964).

6. Robert Michels, *Political Parties: A Sociological Study of the Oligarchical Tendencies of Modern Democracy* (1915; reprint, Glencoe, Ill.: Free Press, 1962), 391.

Chapter 5

1. This logic applies to institutions as well as persons. A preoccupation with bare survival is likely to undermine the group's distinctive character or competence.

2. J. S. Mill, *On Liberty* (London: Routledge, 1991), 74.

3. George Santayana, *The Life of Reason* (1933; reprint, New York: Charles Scribner's Sons, 1954), 258.

4. Ibid., 31.

5. See especially Robert Nozick, *Anarchy, State, and Utopia* (New York: Basic Books, 1974).

6. See John Locke, "An Essay Concerning the True Original, Extent and End of Civil Government," in *Social Contract* (New York: Oxford University Press, 1967), 95.

Chapter 6

1. A remark by Benjamin Disraeli. See *The New Encyclopaedia Britannica* (Chicago: Encyclopaedia Britannica, Inc., 1974), 5:899.

2. See Jeremy Bentham, "Anarchical Fallacies," in *Nonsense upon Stilts*, ed. Jeremy Waldron (New York: Methuen, 1987), 53.

3. Oliver Wendell Holmes, Jr., *The Common Law* (Boston: Little, Brown, 1881), 1.

4. See E. D. Warfield, *The Kentucky Resolutions of 1798* (New York: G. P. Putnam's, 1887), 157.

5. A. V. Dicey, *Introduction to the Study of the Law of the Constitution* (London: Macmillan, 1956), 188.

6. See Kenneth I. Winston, *The Principles of Social Order* (Portland, Oregon: Hart Publishing, 1981), 8.

7. P. J. Proudhon, *Proudhon's Solution of the Social Problem* (1848; reprint, New York: Vanguard, 1927), 45.

8. John Dewey, *Theory of Valuation* (Chicago: University of Chicago Press, 1939), chapter 6.

Chapter 7

1. Robert K. Merton, "Unanticipated Consequences of Purposive Social Action," *American Sociological Review* 1 (1936): 894–904.

2. On bounded rationality, see Herbert Simon, *Models of Man* (John Wiley and Sons, 1957), part 4.

3. Philip Selznick, *Leadership in Administration* (Berkeley: University of California Press, 1957), chapter 3.

4. Ronald Dworkin, *Taking Rights Seriously* (Cambridge, Mass.: Harvard University Press, 1977), chapter 2.

5. This has been called "constrained maximization." See David Gauthier, *Morals by Agreement* (Cambridge: Clarendon Press, 1986), 167–170.

6. Martin Jay, *The Dialectical Imagination* (New York: Little, Brown, 1973).

7. See, for example, John Dewey, *Logic: The Theory of Inquiry* (New York: Holt, 1938), 503ff.

Chapter 8

This chapter is in part adapted from Gertrude Jaeger and Philip Selznick, "A Normative Theory of Culture," *American Sociological Review* 29 (1964).

1. A. L. Kroeber, *Anthropology* (New York: Harcourt, Brace, 1948), 253.

2. Edward Sapir, "Culture: Genuine and Spurious," *American Journal of Sociology* 29 (1924): 402.

3. See Erich Fromm, *Marx's Concept of Man* (New York: Friedrich Ungar, 1961), chapter 5.

4. Karl Marx, *Economical and Philosophical Manuscripts of 1844* (New York: International Publishers, 1964), 107.

5. A. L. Kroeber and Talcott Parsons, "The Concepts of Culture and of Social System," *American Sociological Review* 23 (October 1958): 583.

6. John Dewey, *Art as Experience* (New York: Capricorn Books, 1934), chapter 3.

7. Clyde Kluckhohn, *Culture and Behavior* (New York: Free Press, 1962), 294–295.

8. W. G. Sumner, *Folkways: A Study of the Sociological Importance of Usages, Manners, Customs, Mores, and Morals* (1906; reprint, New York: Mentor Books, 1940), 438.

Chapter 9

1. See Ronald Dworkin, "The Model of Rules," *University of Chicago Law Review* 1 (1946): 35.

2. A. V. Dicey, *Introduction to the Study of the Law of the Constitution* (London: Macmillan, 1956), 188.

3. See Roscoe Pound, *Jurisprudence* (St. Paul, Minn.: West Publishing, 1959), 2:107.

4. *The Thomas Paine Reader* (London: Penguin Books, Ltd., 1987), 266.

5. See M. R. Cohen, *Reason and Nature* (Glencoe, Ill.: Free Press, 1931), 407.

Chapter 10

1. Jean Jacques Rousseau, *The Social Contract* (Chicago: Henry Regnery, 1954), 2.

2. See Hamilton, Madison, and Jay, *The Federalist Papers* (New York: Bantam Books, 1982), nos. 48, 50.

3. F. J. Roethlisberger and William J. Dickson, *Management and the Worker* (Cambridge, Mass.: Harvard University Press, 1947).

Chapter 11

1. *Griswold v. Connecticut*, 318 U.S. 479 (1965).

2. Carol Gilligan, *In a Different Voice: Psychological Theory and Women's Development* (Cambridge, Mass.: Harvard University Press, 1982).

3. This point was noticed by Max Weber in his essay "Politics as a Vocation." Weber contrasted an "ethic of conviction" (*Gesinnungsethik*) with an "ethic of responsibility" (*Verantwortungsethik*). An ethic of responsibility attends to the welfare of a specific person or institution, while an ethic of conviction affirms an idea or principle. See *From Max Weber*, 77–128.

4. *The Federalist* (reprint; New York: Bantam Books, 1987), no. 51.

5. *Thomas Paine Reader*, ed. Michael Foot and Isaac Kramnick (London: Penguin Books, 1987).

6. Philip Selznick, *The Moral Commonwealth* (Berkeley: University of California Press, 1992), 154.

7. Arthur Schlesinger, Jr., *A Thousand Days* (New York: Mariner Books, 2002), 95.

8. Roberto Michels, *Political Parties: A Sociological Study of the Oligarchical Tendencies of Modern Democracy* (1915; reprint, Glencoe, Ill.: Free Press, 1962), 371.

Index

respect, 67, 102; for authority, 47; and comity, 49; for culture, 93; for diversity, 64, 101–2, 134; role in civility, 47, 48, 101; for self, 37, 42, 61, 62, 86, 95, 96, 125; and solidarity, 52–54
Roethlisberger, F. J.: *Management and the Worker*, 127
romanticism, 3, 9; and humanism, 4
Rousseau, Jean-Jacques, 8, 119, 122–23

Santayana, George, 41; on piety, 64; on the realm of spirit, 65
Sapir, Edward: on culture, 94–95
secularization, 26, 95, 120
self, the: formation of, 68–69, 131; ideal vs. contingent/phenomenal, 24, 37; James on, 68; vs. mind, 22, 35; as organic unity, 10; personhood vs. selfhood, 35, 68–70; selfhood of institutions/communities vs. persons, 35
self-determination, 22, 27, 61
self-esteem, 87
self-interest, 20, 42, 111, 126; Durkheim on, 48; as form of rationality, 87–88; and human rights, 51, 74, 130; and public policy, 85; role in economics, 85–86; Tocqueville on, 86; as unregulated, 68; varieties of, 22, 28, 87–88
self-knowledge, 4, 7, 69, 139n1
self-mastery, 26
self-realization, 22, 95
self-regulation, 47
self-respect, 37, 42, 61, 62, 86, 95, 96, 125
self-restraint, 36, 41, 46, 101, 115
self-scrutiny, 34, 73, 78, 135
self-transcendence, 20, 34, 54
separateness vs. interdependence, 67–68
Simmel, Georg, 20

Simon, Herbert: on rationality, 84
Smith, Adam: on the invisible hand, 68, 88
social cohesion, 48, 52, 96, 120, 122, 127, 130
social contract theory, 45–46, 48, 110, 120
socialization: for ideals, 60; as participatory, 70; as repressive, 70
social order: and moral order, 45–55; relationship to freedom, 46, 80
social science: contribution to human well-being, 17; human rights in, 50; and human wholeness and concreteness, 17–18; methodological individualism in, 29–30; normative/humanist inquiry vs. non-normative inquiry, 40; vs. physical science, 19, 20–21, 27; postulate of humanity in, 17–18, 29–30; relationship to history, 27, 127; relationship to humanities, 17, 27, 94–95; relationship to moral philosophy, 27, 28, 29–30, 34, 45, 54–55, 69–70, 85, 119–21, 122–23, 126–27; relationship to qualitative variation, 32; role of function in, 122; role of ideals in, 37–39, 42, 56–58, 129, 135; role of values in, 37–39, 42, 71–81, 93, 129; value-free ideal in, 37–39, 40. *See also* anthropology; economics; jurisprudence; political science; psychology; sociology
sociology, 17, 20, 97, 119–20, 122, 135, 137
Socrates: and Apollo, 4, 7; and humanism, 3, 4–5; on human virtues, 7; on self-knowledge, 4, 7; on the unexamined life, 4
solidarity: vs. individualism, 131–32; and modernization, 95–96; and respect, 52–54